A Passion For
RIBBONRY

Camela Nitschke
A Passion For Ribbonry

Copyright © 1998 by Landauer Corporation

This book was designed and produced by Landauer Books
A division of Landauer Corporation
12251 Maffitt Road, Cumming, Iowa 50061

President and Publisher: Jeramy Lanigan Landauer
Vice President: Becky Johnston
Editor in Chief: Marjon Schaefer
Art Director: Tracy DeVenney
Associate Editors: Sarah Reid, Judith Stern Friedman
Technical Editor: Tricia Coogan
Calligrapher: Cheryl O. Adams
Creative Assistant: Margaret Sindelar
Photographers: Craig Anderson, Dennis Kennedy, Tracy DeVenney
Photos on pages 9 and 11 courtesy of the Bibliothèque Nationale, Paris, France.

Martingale
& COMPANY

Published by Martingale & Company
PO Box 118, Bothell, WA 98041-0118 USA

(Pastimes)
TM

Library of Congress Cataloging-in-Publication Data
Nitschke, Camela, 1948-
    [Passion for Ribbonry]
    Camela Nitschke; A Passion for Ribbonry. -- 1st ed.
        p.   cm.
    Includes index.
    ISBN 1-58477-211-X (pbk.)
    1. Ribbon work. 2. ribbon flowers. I. Title.
  TT850.5.N57 1998
746'.0476--dc21   97-46739
                                                  CIP

10 9 8 7 6 5 4 3 2 1

Camela Nitschke

A Passion For
RIBBONRY

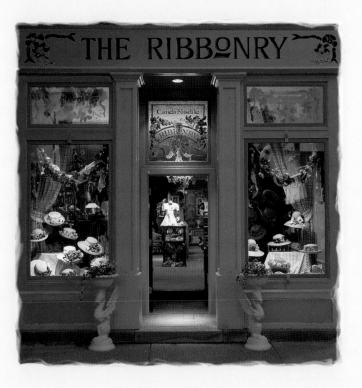

Edited by Marjon Schaefer

Pastimes™

An Imprint of Martingale & Company

Contents

Introduction

Since the dawn of civilization, ribbon has played a significant role in society. As decorative trim on royal banners, it led the way into history-making battles. Lavished on pennants bearing the family crest, it preserved tradition and pageantry. Used on everything, from functional fasteners to fancy adornments, ribbon has had a part in "dressing" our society. Perched atop the heads of respectable Victorian women, ribbon distinguished the genteel from the mundane. As the world advanced and fashion evolved, ribbon was gradually displaced by other textiles, and slowly vanished as an important social statement. Yet few other textiles come close to ribbon's rich history, colorful symbolism, and wonderful versatility.

With *A Passion for Ribbonry*, my desire is to celebrate ribbon—to elevate it to the highly-prized position it deserves. My fascination with ribbon drives nearly all my actions. I've studied French for years to understand the ribbon-makers; traveled to the heart of the French countryside to tour the factories; and returned there to immerse myself in vintage ribbon collections. The bright blaze of flowers from Provence, a result of seasonal rains and hot summer days, inspired me to create lifelike ribbon blooms for home and fashion accents.

It is my hope that *A Passion for Ribbonry* will enhance your appreciation for ribbon as it inspires your own ribbon creations—heirlooms that will preserve the magnificent Ribbon Tradition for generations to come.

Camela Nitschke

Camela Nitschke • Ribbonry

Marie Antoinete
Archiduchasse d'Autriche
Dauphine de France

A Passion for Ribbonry

A Passion for Ribbonry

"Something as exquisite as ribbon surely cannot be allowed to disappear completely."

—Camela Nitschke

Personal Ties

Ribbon has piqued my curiosity since childhood. The annual shopping trip for back-to-school clothing would not have been complete without a visit to the department store for carefully selected ribbons. I chose special ribbons to embellish my dresses—black velvet and dark-color grosgrains to be used at the collar, hem, or cuffs—and brightly colored plaid and

watered-silk floral ribbons for my hair. After serving their purpose, the worn and frayed plaid taffeta ribbons which tied up my ponytail were reinvented, with a stitch here and a pleat there, into sashes and trims for the doll clothes I created from my mother's scrap bag.

On long car rides, when fabric and ribbon were not available, my clever mother encouraged my interest in design and provided entertainment… with only a roll of aluminum foil, I molded and wrapped my dolls in every imaginable fashion.

At seven years of age, my favorite dress was one my mother made for me to wear at Christmas. The velvet skirt was striped with shimmering jewel-tone satin ribbons, giving the whole creation a magical appearance.

Later, my one-of-a-kind dresses for proms featured ribbon embellishments combined with such fine fabrics as voile, organdy, and piqué.

When visiting my grandmother and great aunts in Canada, a tea party out under the tree was a tradition. Often, they'd reminisce about favorite party dresses, and riding via sleigh to fancy

Degas' painting of a hatmaker is a captivating portrait of society's enduring passion for ribbon.

winter balls. The lively stories were quite entertaining, but the detailed descriptions of their French ballgowns captured my attention. A few remnants of these dresses, proof of a bygone and elegant era, could be found in an old trunk in the attic.

In this treasure-trove, pleated soft-color ribbon rosettes adorned delicate satin dancing pumps to complement the pastel gowns worn to coming-out parties. The gowns had obviously been passed around, but all had distinct embellishments: a ruched flower here, a ribbon there, or trim tacked-on to ease the fit. I recall that one gown even had a fish-tail pleated flounce. My relatives clearly followed the styles, but adapted the dresses to match their personalities. Along with generations of cousins, I was privileged to play dress-up and reveled in the faded glory of those ballgowns.

That early fascination with fancy garments grew into an interest in fashion and design. By my teen years, I cut pictures from catalogs and fashion magazines, adapting them to outfits of my own creation, using my room as a design studio. I was always busy planning, experimenting with colors, and yearning for lessons at an art museum.

In fact, ribbon even influenced my wedding—I chose to wear ribbon instead of a veil, with a blue satin bow artfully framing my face.

Launched on a new course—balancing the demands of marriage and small children— I preserved a sense of self by pursuing my interests in ribbon, art, and French.

Fortuitously, on a trip with my husband to Dallas, Texas, we saw woven-ribbon belts which inspired me to make my own and market them in nearby stores. All the money I made was reinvested in buying ribbons. I purchased imported weaves from Grayblock in New York, and traveled there once a year to lose myself in the ribbon warehouses. For me, ribbon became an art form as I wove it into beautiful patterns and so continued to look for new possibilities.

To complement my craft, I studied abstract art, French language, and history. Courses in French literature especially introduced me to 17th- and 18th-century society, where I found detailed descriptions of what the nobility was wearing. The writings of Madame de Sévigné proved a valuable source of information: In an effort to keep her daughter appraised of the latest fashions at the court of Louis XIV, she wrote lengthy letters with colorful and accurate accounts.

One of a unique series of occupational engravings, this one shows the rubaniere plying her trade.

A Passion for Ribbonry

On side-trips to the French countryside I developed a fondness for wildflowers which, in turn, inspired me to write this book.

In addition, studies of the paintings of 17th- and 18th-century artists such as Boucher, Drouais, and Fragonard provided an in-depth view of dress and lifestyles that featured ribbon.

Whatever I read prompted further learning. While absorbed in the detailed descriptions of costumes, the use of ribbon for ornamentation, and the paintings of stately noblemen and women, I discovered that my interests in the language, art, and ribbons of France were all connected.

Weaving a History

Passionately, I set out on a mission to uncover the story of ribbon—how it began, how it was used, who made it, who wore it, and how it became such an integral part of French society.

At home in Perrysburg, Ohio, my resources were limited. I delved into every piece of literature I could find only to discover little documentation.

So…my husband and I flew to France, the heart of the ribbon industry, to peruse actual samples in French museums, study the books, learn the rich culture, and chronicle ribbon's development. (Of course, other countries were making ribbon as well; however, France is responsible for its widespread distinction.)

I learned that in its infancy, ribbon was more functional than decorative, being used to secure clothing and other articles. Records dating back as early as 700 B.C. describe broad bows on the capes of Parthian women. In Greece, ribbon was intertwined with reeds for molding. And during the Middle Ages, ribbons were used as tie-backs on canopy beds.

It was not until silk-weaving arrived in Avignon, France, that ribbon began to flourish. After the Romans conquered Gaul in the 14th century, Avignon became a favorite vacation spot. The Mediterranean climate encouraged hearty crops of mulberry trees, the silk worm's only food, which in turn stimulated the production of luxurious silk.

When church nobility moved to Avignon by order of the French king, silk demand grew even greater. The popes would dress in ornate gold-edged ribbons and elaborate brocades to distinguish their rank, then proudly parade down city streets. In 1466, King Louis XI was the first to invite Italian weavers to teach their skills to the people of Lyon, a commercial center on the Rhone and Saone rivers, but the project was unsuccessful.

Instead, silk-weaving looms and narrower single-piece ribbon looms were set up in the city of Tours, near the King's royal chateaux along the Loire. Nevertheless, the presence of the court in Lyon during the Italian wars made Lyon a logical center of silk production.

Later, King Francis I, influenced by the ornate Italian styles, encouraged his court to dress accordingly. Men and women bedecked themselves in lavish clothing, often fashioned from nothing but trimmings. Embroidered ribbons were given as gifts, or "faveurs," to worthy nobility. Even the horses wore bridles and girdles in crisscrossed bands of ribbon.

Finally in 1523, King Francis I successfully chartered Italian and Syrian artisans to teach their weaving skills to the Lyonese. By 1560, as many as 5,000 workers were weaving silk and ribbon to accommodate the demand for extravagant dress.

Lyon continued as the production center for larger silk goods, while its neighbors, the Velay Region and St. Etienne, about 45 miles to the south, were awarded the ribbon charters. And thus began a thriving cottage industry that would last for over 400 years.

Secrets Revealed in St. Etienne

I visited the town of St. Etienne, which looks much the same as it did centuries ago. At the Museum of Art and Industry—the only museum dedicated to ribbons—I pored over a million glorious ribbon samples made in this historic town.

I was privileged to become acquainted with ribbon historian and museum curator Madame Nadine Besse. Her dedicated research, visible throughout her many books and articles about the ribbons of

Permanently at rest, ribbon looms from the 17th century are displayed in the world's only museum dedicated to ribbons —the Museum of Art and Industry in St. Etienne, France.

A Passion for Ribbonry

At the Museum of Art and Industry in St. Etienne, I share the view from the balcony with Mme. Nadine Besse, noted ribbon historian and the museum's curator.

St. Etienne, has greatly contributed to the literature. Through the museum's extensive archives of primarily 18th-century ribbon samples I have been able to focus on several different design trends.

I learned about Pierre Rossipon, St. Etienne's first recorded ribbon-maker in 1517, who likely worked for a Lyon silk manufacturer. As did other master weavers of the time, Rossipon collected silk thread from the manufacturers, which he then took back to his atelier, or workshop, attached to his house. Here, he wove ribbons on a low-warp loom, a manual operation producing only one pattern at a time. When completed, Rossipon took the ribbon billots, or reels, back to the manufacturer, in exchange for another lot of silk.

By 1660, St. Etienne and its surrounding provinces boasted 8,000 ribbon looms and 370 passementiers (those who make "fancy edging").

I was further entranced by the exquisite products of this time when I discovered the Cardinal Richelieu collection, a rare accounting of 17th-century woven goods, now housed in the Bibliotheque Nationale in Paris. This national treasure was compiled during the reign of Louis XIII and comprises seven leather-bound volumes.

The books are accessible only by government approval and prearranged appointments. After much persistence and many phone calls, I finally was granted permission to view the books which provided great inspiration for my own ribbon revival.

The Richelieu collection offers not only a wealth of pictures and actual ribbon samples, but describes in detail how the ribbons were made, how they were used on costumes, and from which country they came. Influenced by the blossoming trade with China and the East Indies, the designs were bold and brightly colored. There were stripes, Bhuta flowers, passion flowers, and even a Tree of Life, used mainly for the court. Pale yellow, gray, and clear blues added to traditional reds and forest greens created fabrics and ribbons of spectacular pattern and shape. Great artists such as Jean Revel, Phillipe de la Salle, and Jean

Pillement also influenced the Lyonese silk designers, who, in turn, greatly inspired the inventive use of ribbon.

The Height of Ribbon Fashion

Demand for ribbons continued throughout the 17th century, the period which many consider ribbon's most elegant era. Louis XIV wore jewel-trimmed ribbons even on his shoes! He encouraged his court to be creative in their dress.

In one instance, during a formal hunt at Fontainbleau, Mlle. de Fontanges is noted to have used her ribbon garter to tie up her tousled hair. In her coy effort to be more presentable to the king, she launched a fashion trend which continues to this day, commonly referred to as a chignon or French knot.

Under Louis XV, Rococo styles departed from order and rules, and instead reflected imagination and fanciful forms. Clothing became looser and more free-flowing when Mme. de Montespon (Louis XV's mistress) popularized the robe volant—a dress characterized by loose back pleats and an informal style which she wore to keep her pregnancies secret and thus avoid court gossip.

Ribbons adorned every possible fashion aspect. Narrow, looped bows trimmed the shoulders, sleeves, and cuffs of ladies' dresses. Often, a large bow or ribbon rosette was attached to the dress bodice and aptly named parfait contentment, or perfectly content. Likewise, men's clothing was embellished with flots and touffes—bunches of bows at the waist, shoulders, knees, cuffs, and hat.

During the reign of Louis XVI, circa 1784, fashion was celebrated in its highest form. Designers such as Rose Bertin and Mme. Eloffe devoted themselves to elaborate dress, hat, and coiffure creations. Marie Antoinette was the ultimate trend-setter, singlehandedly driving the polished, high society of that time to new heights of fashion. Ribbons were ruffled, ruched, and gathered in a variety of ways, and even made to resemble lace. Dresses dripped with ribbons, jewels, and feathers, and, in obvious excess, were combined with live flowers. Low

Fashion plates, such as these from the 19th century, depict lavish applications of ribbon trims on garments and accessories.

15

necklines, wide hoops, or paniers, and lavish adornments epitomized women's costume.

Ribbon's influence can be seen in 18th and 19th-century court paintings which I have learned to view from an entirely new perspective. In a painting by Boucher, for instance, Madame de Pompadour is shown wearing a beautiful ribbon collier, or necklace.

In another, Marie Antoinette poses in a ribbon-enhanced stomacher—a detachable front piece with several rows of decreasing-size bows, referred to as an echelle of ribbons. I enjoy replicating these old ribbon usages,

In the French Court, Marie Antoinette exemplified the height of fashion. Here she is adorned with an echelle of ribbons—a detachable front piece decorated with several rows of decreasing-size bows.

especially in the bridal items currently featured in The Ribbonry.

Ribbon's Last Hurrah

Already essential to fashion, ribbon subsequently conveyed symbolism in its colors and use. For instance, when a well-known lawyer was involved in a social scandal and forced to leave Paris, striped ribbon became the rage, symbolic of being "struck off a list."

Events of the court and topics of the day provided inspiration for other outlandish creations. When Louis XVI was inoculated for smallpox, Rose Bertin, famous designer to Marie Antoinette, incorporated polka-dot ribbons into a bonnet as a tribute to triumph over smallpox. (Survivors of the dreaded disease wore smallpox spots almost as a badge of honor).

The revocation of the Edict of Nantes in 1685 interrupted France's flourishing ribbon industry. Religious persecution forced nearly 60,000 non-Catholic weavers and dyers to leave the country. Many fled to Basle, Switzerland, which for the next 200 years, would grow to become a ribbon-weaving hub, along with Krefeld, Germany; Vienna, Austria; and Coventry, England.

This expansion threatened St. Etienne's livelihood but created the impetus for technological advances.

Switzerland's 1786 invention of the bar loom, or Zurich loom, modernized the ribbon-weaving process, and made it possible to weave 36 pieces of ribbon at one time.

By the dawning of the Revolution in 1789, ribbon came to play an important political role—that of distinguishing citizens from the hated nobility. Once a simple costume trim, the cocarde, a multi-looped circular ornament, now became a symbol of the Revolution. Men, women, and children were forced to wear the cocarde in their hats and clothing to tout the new republican Tricolore—blue, white, and red.

During the Continental Blockade under the first Empire, the industry faced some difficulty obtaining raw materials; however, apart from this snag, ribbon enjoyed its Golden Age.

The invention of the jacquard loom in the early 1800s enabled weaving of double-faced ribbons in widths up to seven inches. With its computer-like card system, the loom could replicate in ribbon souvenir black-and-white photographs and engravings that documented elaborate designs.

Advancements in silk production through the use of electricity and steam also affected silk ribbon. In St. Etienne, yarn-dyed ribbons, rather than piece dyed, led to a demand for new colors and tints, leading to a

vibrant chemical industry which continues to this day.

With contemporary tools at hand, ribbon-making was as elaborate as ever; yet rapidly changing fashions began to threaten its very existence.

To compete with the popularity of feathers, for example, ribbon was woven to picture a quill, as shown above, with the cross-weave cut to resemble soft feathered edges. Other patterns included paisley (1850s), moiré or watered-silk ribbon, see below, and cut-velvet or sabre ribbon, named after the knife that cuts the design.

Dramatic new fashions and fierce competition from Switzerland and

A Passion for Ribbonry

Germany pressured French ribbon-makers like never before. In addition, the American Civil War imposed excessive duties on imports, and consumers demanded less costly goods.

To cope with declining business, manufacturers turned to producing exquisite, one-of-a-kind ribbons. However, luxury items alone could not support the French ribbon industry and one by one, companies disappeared, which leaves only a handful of ribbon manufacturers today, St. Etienne being the home of one of them.

At the 150-year-old Julien Faure Industries, antique motor-driven jacquard looms can produce up to 15 designs at a time; however, set-up for

Visiting with Mr. Daniel Faure and touring his family's 150-year old ribbon factory certainly was the highlight of one of my latest research trips to France.

each one can take weeks and intricate ribbon designs are reserved for the few remaining master weavers.

Having visited the factory on numerous occasions, I have come to know several great-grandsons of the company's founder. During one of my visits, Mr. Daniel Faure explained how to distinguish quality ribbons from ordinary ones. Faure Industries binds their ribbon edges with an interwoven lock stitch. Other manufacturers cut costs by heat-bonding or gluing the selvedge edges, making them more inclined to ravel.

While Faure Industries certainly has progressed over the years, two things prevail: the company's meticulous design skills and the painstaking production of nothing less than ribbon of the finest quality. The company has produced historic patterns for restorations of Versailles and other recognizable chateaux. It also produces personal labels and luxurious fabrics for today's most fashionable designers.

Planting Seeds

Over the course of many years traveling, studying, and exploring the French culture, I have acquired an assortment of vintage ribbons. Rather than allow them to gather dust and become forgotten, I prefer to find uses that will not only showcase their

distinct and varying beauty but also ensure their lasting value.

My mother and I opened a shop called Ribbon Alley. This melange of blouses, t-shirts, and wrap-around skirts—all adorned with my ribbon creations—succeeded with the help of nine busy seamstresses.

Six years later, however, I tired of the special orders. With the births of our third and fourth children, I took over our dining room, where ribbon soon overflowed the table, floors, and any other surface. In 1987, I moved into a studio we built in our backyard, which became a wonderful retreat. Inspired by Monet's lush wildflower gardens, I planted flowers, all the while experimenting with ribbons.

Meanwhile, I continued my studies of French culture. I discovered Frenchman Charles Rebour, who is considered the best ribbon artist of his time (1860–1880). Born in 1831, Rebour lived in Paris with his parents on the Rue des Celestins. After defacing a carriage with a lovely landscape (early graffiti!), Rebour was "rescued" by artist M. Duval, who believed he had talent and who took him on as an art student. Thereafter, Rebour studied with various instructors, but he was most inspired by the wildflowers of the countryside. Rather than sketching in a stuffy studio, he opted for the gardens of

While visiting Faure Industries, I marveled at the intricate and complex workings of the large ribbon-weaving looms.

Paris and Luxembourg Palace. While attending a fine-arts school at age 16, Rebour won the King's Prize, which would have allowed him to travel in pursuit of sketching, but Charles declined the award for personal reasons.

Rather, he left Paris to join M. M. Collard et Comte, one of St. Etienne's most respected ribbon houses. Having suffered from the plague of 1847, Rebour was an invalid and settled in the Forez region, where he remained for more than 50 years. While convalescing at Sail-Sous-Couzan, he filled his sketchbooks with images of the countryside.

Rebour lent his talents to several ribbon houses, including the house of Granger and Rebour, which he founded with M. M. Gemier et Frecon in 1856; the Societé Caquet, Vauzelle et Ducote of Lyon; and Cognet and Gerentet, which he headed until his death in 1897.

One might wonder how one man could have influenced ribbon-making so dramatically. In fact, it is his work

which makes up many of the splendid samples in the Museum of Art and Industry. One of his contemporaries wrote: "Charles Rebour was a studied artist in the most elevated sense of the word. He lived for the joy of creating and seemed to breathe his very soul into his work." Rebour translated his love of flowers into the threads of the best silk available. Using intense blues, rare greens, and passionate purples, Rebour's work resembled the stained-glass windows of the 12th and 13th centuries. His signature technique of distressing the ribbon by leaving out the crosswise weave made the vibrant colors sing. Cornflowers, poppies, daisies, buttercups, forget-me-nots, and even dandelions magically swayed through the delicate weave.

Interestingly, while Rebour was "growing" his gardens in silk, Claude Monet was cultivating them on canvas.

An avid horticulturist, Monet was committed to preserving indigenous wildflowers, an interest he shared with his friend and mentor, and famous botanist, Edouard André. I visited Monet's gardens at Giverny (some 50 miles outside Paris), where Monet spent forty-three years of his life, beginning in 1883.

Like Rebour, Monet was keen on simple shapes and bold colors. Influenced by the shape of Holland's bulb fields, Monet designed a series of long, rectangular paint-box beds. Here he experimented with composition, light, and color. He was opposed to black and earth tones, and preferred combinations of yellow and blue, or red and yellow, although he never mixed colors in the same bed. Sunflowers, dahlias, gladiolas, jonquil, poppies, and Christmas rose were among his favorite flowers to paint.

For both great artists, wildflowers were an endless source of motifs—the perfect, natural models. They were nature enthusiasts who appreciated the color and texture of wildflowers, and how they captured light.

"Charles Rebour is the true master of the industry who raised the profession to the highest level of competence and dignity…. His collection of sample ribbons will be the best story of the ribbon manufacture of St. Etienne."

— Guy Chastel, Editions Musee d'Art et d'Industrie,
Ville de Saint-Etienne

Budding New Course

Suddenly, my work related to the accomplishments of these men, which then allowed me to explore a new dimension in ribbon. I began twisting, folding, and stitching the ribbon to emulate the wildflowers I saw in St. Etienne, also now blooming outside my studio. My ribbons gained more than a decorative purpose; they also would heighten my appreciation of nature. I, too, turned to my garden as an open-air studio.

Using ribbon, I replicate lupine, foxglove, and poppies. I also have included flowers that are indigenous to America, such as the sunflower, coreopsis, and gaillardia. When climate or conditions do not permit, I consult my library of botanical books.

In any case, I aim to capture the essence of flowers' form and texture. Focusing on indigenous and endangered species, I strive for accuracy in my interpretation so I can preserve these miraculous products of our earth. Ribbonry for me has become not only a craft, but a true art form.

Encouraged by this new direction, I returned to retail and, in 1990, opened The Ribbonry. The facade of the 130-year-old building received a face-lift to celebrate historic Perrysburg. Inside, the shop resembles an authentic 18th-century French boutique.

Designed after the Palais Royale, a popular social spot in Paris, The Ribbonry harkens back to the 1730s, when ribbon enjoyed its greatest glory. A gold chandelier, rows of moss green cabinets, and beautiful ribbon things fill the place. Using my research to authenticate the designs—both in the store's decor and in the ribbons—I hope to put ribbon back

Reminiscent of the shape of Holland's bulb fields, Monet's flower beds are a series of long, rectangular boxes.

on its pedestal. From a wedding dress in the style of Marie Antoinette to a ribbon kit that enables you to create the flowers…I hope to revive the resplendence of ribbons that otherwise might be lost.

Lasting Fabric

With *A Passion For Ribbonry,* you, too, can appreciate the Ribbon Tradition. While history testifies to ribbon's valued place in society, its shape and form continues to evolve. Beyond its place in fashion, ribbon shows up on furniture, wallpaper, lampshades, pillows, picture hangers, ornaments, garlands, and so on.

Consider this book to be a "ribbon ceremony" of sorts to help you recognize ribbon's remarkable legacy. I've spent a lifetime following its tracks through the sprawling French countryside, museums, books, and

Seeding the open fields behind my workshop with hundreds of Monet-inspired wildflowers, was the impetus to advance my ribbon work to new and undiscovered heights.

the cobbled streets of St. Etienne. Together, the master ribbon weavers, the Richelieu collection, Charles Rebour, and even Claude Monet, create a wonderful tapestry—yet every twist of ribbon reveals new and exciting possibilities.

You'll find, when making projects from this book, that ribbonry is a wonderfully accessible art form. I am not a trained seamstress, nor do I follow conventional sewing rules; rather, I believe in free interpretation. All you need are a few simple tools, a little patience, and imagination.

Ribbon—tuck it, twist it, pin it, pull it, and experiment with the magical folds of color. The ideas presented here are designed to build an unlimited ribbon-flower repertoire. Whether a small corsage, bouquet, pillow embellishment, or ambitious wildflower quilt, the results become valued heirlooms, sure to please present as well as future generations.

Seemingly small, such sumptuous ornamentations hold the promise of a significant niche in the textile trends and traditions of the future.

My visits to Monet's Giverny proved to be an enchanting form of research that many a scholar would envy!

The Ribbonry

The Ribbonry

Welcome to The Ribbonry in Perrysburg, Ohio, a classic example and perfect blend of cultural harmony. In 1990, the 130-year-old building, an ensemble of French and American architecture, was renovated on the outside to celebrate historic Perrysburg. Inside, owner Camela Nitschke has painstakingly recreated an authentic 18th-century French boutique which captures the essence of the Palais Royale, a popular social spot in Paris.

The return to a gentler era begins with the turn of an ornate brass knob on the front entry door. Visitors are ushered into a breathtaking recreation of a rubaniere's shop from the 1730's, the period of ribbon's greatest glory.

A glistening gold chandelier presides over an elegant array of antique mirrors, cabinets, and hat stands—the background for "all things ribbon" that spill over from the moss-green cabinets lining the walls and cascade in a wash of color to the floor below.

The Ribbonry

Piled higher than Madame de Pompadour's tresses, ribbon-embellished pillows take on the form of a unique art piece. Simple techniques for ribbon-weaving, folding, and pleating. can turn plump pillows into visual demonstrations of the versatility of ribbon.

In addition, mixing widths, types, and styles; and plaids, solids, and stripes of scraps of ribbon makes the woven pillow front an economical final resting place for favorite ribbons used in various projects throughout the year!

The ultimate tribute to the endless decorating options with ribbon, a shadowbox displaying purple coneflowers and black-eyed Susans crafted from ribbons, becomes a spectacular showcase when matted with a wide, checkered ribbon and topped off with an inexpensive gold frame.

An ordinary purchased lampshade trimmed with ribbon pansies and a triple box-pleated edging becomes an instant conversation piece as the crowning glory of a designer lampbase.

The Ribbonry

Perched atop a glass shelf in one of the shop's showcases, a ribbon-framed bouquet of blue flag iris is complemented by the vibrant hues of ribbon-woven and floral-bedecked pillows—each a work of ribbon art!

The impressive antique French case at right lends authenticity to the revival of 1730's romance at The Ribbonry and becomes a beautiful backdrop for a waterfall of exquisite antique and reproduction ribbons.

Violet

Camela's Workshop

Camela's Workshop

arden flowers galore and a vivid purple clematis topiary greet Camela each summer morning at the door of her charming cottage workshop. Soft morning sunlight filtering through the multi-paned windows lends an air of tranquility to this serene setting.

Surrounded by the glorious ribbons that inspire floral masterpieces such as this trio of ribbon-trimmed hats, Camela spends many pleasantly productive hours in her ribbon designer's dream world.

It is here, surrounded "by every loveliness of nature and every luxury of art," as Henry James observed, that Camela makes her mark on the world as she pursues her passion for ribbonry.

Morning Glory

Fresh-picked vintage roses, cultivated by a local gardener, are gentle reminders of a bygone era, when women sought shelter from the sun under the broad brim of a straw skimmer. Hats that offer present-day comfort like the one shown opposite, are popular fashion accents when trimmed with a perky bow and silk ribbon flower.

After a day of designing in her restful workshop retreat, Camela's scrap basket brims with lengths of leftover ribbon. They're put to good use in the ribbon-woven fabric that graces a reproduction French chair.

"Ribbonry for me has become not only a craft, but a true art form."

The Garden Room

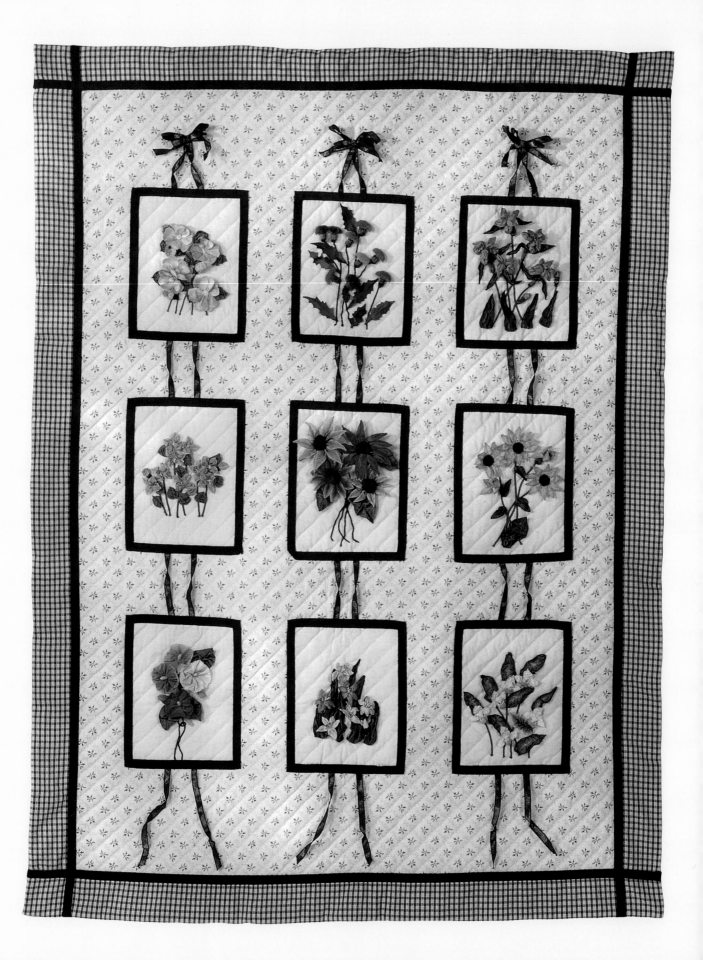

The Garden Room

Imagine a breakfast or dining room immediately transformed into an old-fashioned French garden room when filled with ribbon-flower artistry. In Camela's home, a soaring high-ceiling space and a wide expanse of windows and walls becomes the perfect setting for showcasing her spectacular wall quilt that is detailed in the Step-by-Step section beginning on page 98.

Poppies, showy lady's slippers, sunflowers, and cosmos entwine with grapevines woven through the chandelier to literally light up the room!

The Garden Room

Reflections of Camela's artistry, the ribbon flowers and plaid bows that trim the mirror are intermingled with dried eucalyptus, moss, and other naturals. The lupines, Johnny jump-ups, tiger lilies, and daisies then repeat in larger scale on the dramatic wreath displayed on the sun-swathed transom above doors that open to a flower-filled courtyard (see page 46). Camela's choice of a color palette for the garden room was inspired by the many visits she has made to Monet's gardens in Giverney, France.

Pastels that range from light periwinkle blue to purple and from sunny yellow to deepest gold blend into a spectacular ribbon-flower bouquet, opposite. Featured among the lilies and black eyed Susans is the lupine, an unusual blue flower which also happens to have the distinction of being one of Camela's all-time favorites as well as one of the most challenging flowers to replicate in ribbon.

Lupine

The Garden Room

Wreathed in splendor, the light-filled space offers an early morning sanctuary as soft rays of sunlight filter through double sets of French doors and gently reappear for a late afternoon encore.

Quiet elegance for the garden room calls for the calming blue and white of the draperies that frame the French doors and are tied back with a pleated-ribbon frivolité—a confection of Camela's own creation.

"The bright blaze of flowers from Provence inspired me to create lifelike ribbon blooms."

Les Petites

Les Petites

Diminutive ribbon-trimmed hats that grace the garden gate are just the right size for your little girl's favorite 18-inch doll.

Here, five tiny bonnets perch precariously on an antique hat stand, forming a circular cluster of eye-catching floral arrangements. These miniature versions of Camela's full-size flowers, including the vintage rose, zinnia, morning glory, and chou rose, are all worked in narrow widths of ribbon. Some of the tiny florets, such as the chamomile and dog violet, Camela designed exclusively for her millinery-in-miniature are explained in full detail on pages 118–129. Can you envision a small cluster on your lapel?

May Weed

Romantic Retreat

Camela's creative ribbon accents resonate in the romantic retreat shown here—the ultimate in suite dreams!

Center stage, the fabulous fabric-draped bed canopy boasts sumptuous ribbon garlands in full bloom. Nestled in the soft folds of the canopy's fabric layers, a ribbon-framed bouquet of Camela's Virginia roses adds to the three-dimensional effect and achieves the balance so important to the French romanticists of the early 18th century.

A lady's dressing table, left, can be a fashion statement all its own with ribbon lavished on everything from the pleated-trim lampshade and woven photo frame to the ribbon-flower wreaths holding the swag.

Tie the ensemble together by weaving ribbons through latticework on vintage linens or a series of button-holes stitched on pillow fronts like the ones shown on the next two pages.

Sweet Pea

Romantic Retreat

Finishing touches for Camela's romantic bedroom include the fanciful frivolité, left. Used as a dainty door decor or displayed in a difficult to decorate corner, it adds quick-and-easy dashes of coordinating color to the room. This perfectly pleated accent piece is merely a clever combination of the cocarde with a galette, tied together with a picot-edge satin ribbon.

For additional small-scale accessorizing, cover round or oval boxes with wide gingham or moiré ribbons; knotted bands of French ombré ribbon add a festive air. Crown the box lids with clusters of petit fleurs such as pansies, cabochon roses, and violets. Leaves in various shades of green, crafted from satin and taffeta ribbons, anchor the floral fantasies and provide a framework for the flowers' gentle pastel colors.

All of these accessories easily lend themselves to serve as charming gifts, pretty party centerpieces and stylish ornaments on a dresser or mantel.

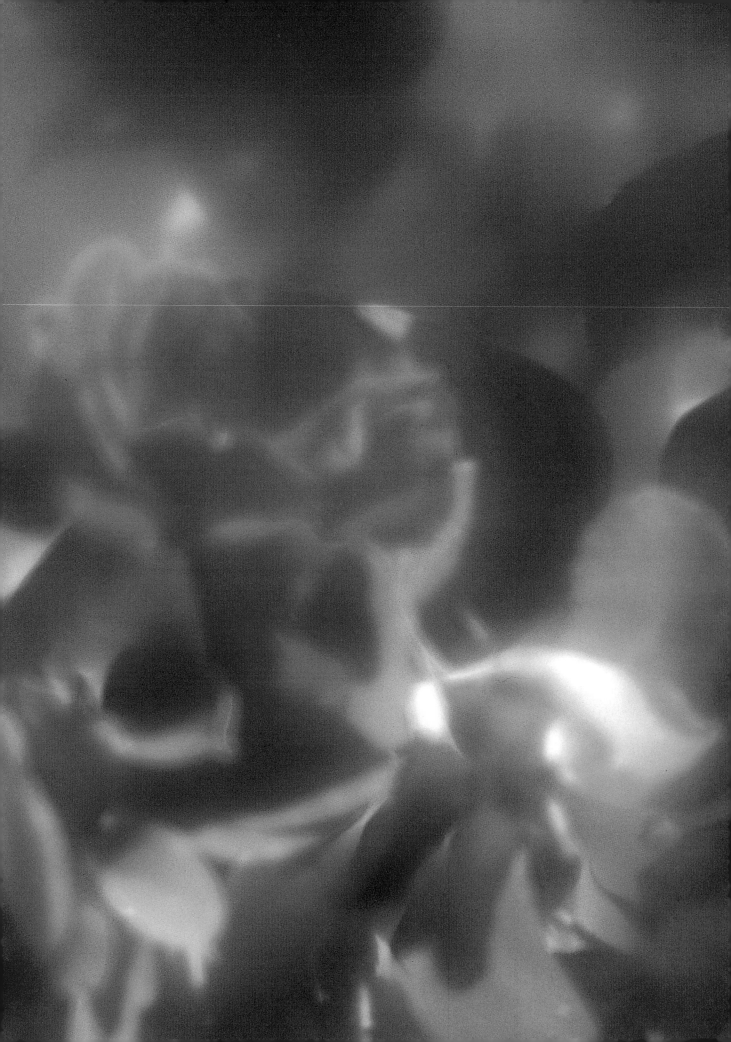

Couture

Couture

Every little girl's dream dress can be just that much more memorable with a floral accent for the satin-ribbon sash. Pastel roses and a trio of pods festoon the center of the sash closure, left. The versatile pods highlight the picot-edge ribbon bow, below left, as well as the charming corsage, above right.

Other fashion inspirations that work up quickly are the satin waterfall necktie, below, which is

"My dresses featured ribbon embellishments combined with such fabrics as voile and piqué."

accented with chou roses and embellished with ribbon embroidery, and the old-fashioned posy pin, button covers, and ribbon cascade pin shown on the blouse and vest, right.

Let the detailed step-by-step photographs on the following pages be your guide to making any or all these flowers—mix and match to your heart's content!

Zinnia

Step-by-Step

Step-by-Step

Follow along with Camela as she takes you into the wonderful world of wildflowers—ribbon wildflowers that is. Every flower has minutely detailed instructions and, since a picture speaks a thousand words, colorful photographs to illustrate each step to success. The materials that are listed in the large bordered Materials box were used to make the flower that is shown on that page. It is not at all necessary to use exactly the same ribbon styles though—a different color or width will produce an equally lovely flower. Just make sure that when you change the width you also change the length so the proportions will still work. Camela often picks ribbons for their color; if these happen to be wire-edge ribbons, she removes the wires from the selvedges and discards them. Her goal is to create lifelike flowers; however, don't hesitate to be creative and construct your own fantasy versions.

 For fun flower applications, closely study the accessories in the photographs on the previous pages.

Zinnia

The zinnias we see today are very different from the original species. Plant breeders have transformed the wildflower into myriad varieties out of the seeds that were collected in Mexico by an 18th-century German botanist.

MATERIALS

- 1½ yards of 1"-wide white organdy ribbon

- Stamens

- 3" square of buckram

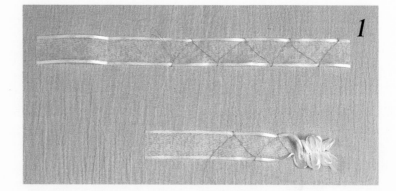

1. Mark bottom selvedge at 2" intervals. Mark top selvedge at 2" intervals, starting 1" from the end. Beginning at top selvedge and using a double thread, take three stitches toward next mark on bottom selvedge. Carry next stitch around the selvedge and take three stitches toward next interval on top selvedge. Carry a stitch around selvedge and repeat process across ribbon. Pull thread tight, gathering ribbon to an 11" length; knot thread.

2. Gather a bunch of stamens. Fold the bunch in half and wrap it with thread or stem wire.

3. Place the stamens at the end of the gathered ribbon and coil three of the petal-shape gathers around them. Secure in place; then secure to the center of the buckram. Coil the remaining ribbon around the center, tacking the selvedges of the inner petals to the buckram as you go. Trim the buckram close to the stitching in back.

Cherokee Rose

Rosa laevigatae

This semi-hardy plant which produces single flowers has become naturalized in the United States. They were originally part of a very small group of roses discovered in China.

MATERIALS

- 25" of 1½"-wide pink shaded wire-edge ribbon for one flower and one pod

- 10" of 1"-wide green wire-edge ribbon for large leaf

- 8" of 1"-wide green wire-edge ribbon for medium leaf

- 3" square of buckram

- 3" square of felt

- Small amount of stuffing

- Green stem wire

- Stamens

- Pin back

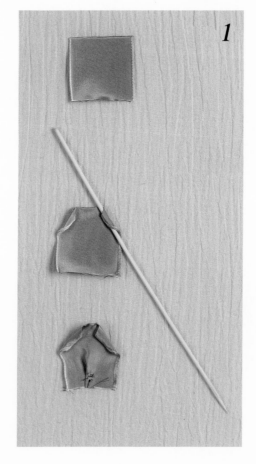

1. Cut seven 3" pieces and one 4" piece of pink shaded ribbon. Set aside the 4" piece. Fold each 3" piece in half widthwise. With the fold at top, curl the top corners of one piece by rolling them onto a thin wooden skewer— you get a very neat and elegant curl with a wooden roller like the one shown. A plastic or metal knitting needle will do, but the ribbon rolls easier on wood. Next, make a ¼" pleat in the center of the lower edge of the petal and secure with a couple of stitches. Make seven petals.

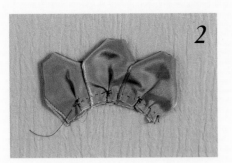

2. With the petals overlapping each other about a quarter of the width of each petal, use a running stitch to join seven petals ¼" from the cut edges. Connect the first petal to the last petal.

6. Fold the 10" and 8" pieces of green ribbon in half widthwise. Fold down the top corners as shown in the photo below. With double thread, sew a small running stitch up the diagonal edge with the cut end, along the top edge and down the opposite diagonal edge. Pull up the thread slightly, but do not finish it off. Open the layers and arrange the gathers carefully, keeping most of them in the center and toward the bottom of the leaf. When you are happy with leaf's shape, secure the thread with two or three stitches in the seam. Sew the leaves to the buckram behind the flower. Trim the buckram and felt squares to 1½" circles. Sew a pin back to the felt; sew to the buckram.

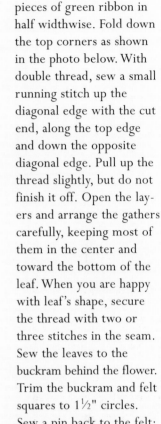

3. Pull the thread tightly to almost close the center of the flower, leaving just enough room to poke the stamens through. Sew the flower to the buckram square.

4. Secure a small bundle of stamens in the center by wrapping them with thread. Sew the wrapped center of the bundle to the center of the flower and to the buckram. Fluff out the stamens.

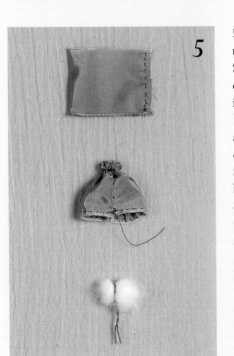

5. Fold the 4" piece of pink ribbon in half widthwise. Sew together ¼" from the cut edges; turn seam to the inside. Sew a running stitch ¼" below the top selvedge and pull thread tight to create a ruffle; knot thread. Sew a running stitch near bottom selvedge; leave open. Loop a piece of stem wire around the stuffing and insert stuffing into pod. Pull gathers around stuffing; knot thread. Trim stem to 1" and bend the ends. Hook stem to the buckram just behind the flower.

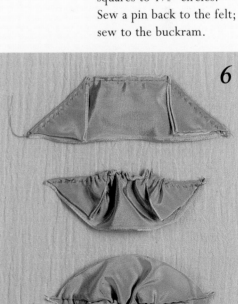

Daisy

Chrysanthemum leucanthemum

This attractive woody perennial grows in moist soils in sun or semi-shade. You will find the sunny yellow and white blooms appear all summer in prairies and fields. As you can see from its latin name, the daisy is really a chrysanthemum.

MATERIALS

- 1¾ yards of 1"-wide white wire-edge taffeta.

- 7" of ⅝"-wide yellow grosgrain

- 7" of ⅝"-wide green grosgrain

- 3" square of buckram

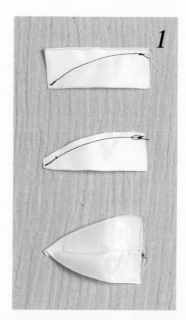

1. Cut eleven 5" pieces of white taffeta. Fold each piece in half widthwise. Using small running stitches or machine straight stitches, sew diagonally across the ribbon in a curved fashion. Secure thread with a few backstitches; clip thread. Trim ribbon to ⅛" from seam. Seal cut edges with clear nail polish to prevent fraying. Open ribbons up into petals.

2. Use a running stitch to join eleven petals ¼" from the cut edges. Connect the first petal to the last petal.

3. Pull the thread tightly to close the center of the flower. Arrange the petals. Sew the flower to the center of the buckram square.

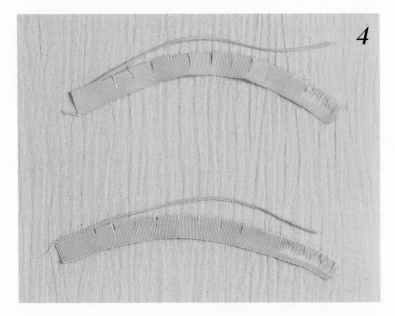

4. Trim each piece of grosgrain to $\frac{3}{8}$"-wide by cutting off one selvedge. Every $\frac{1}{2}$", make a perpendicular cut to within $\frac{1}{8}$" from the selvedge. Using a pin or an awl, pull out the threads to create a fringed strip.

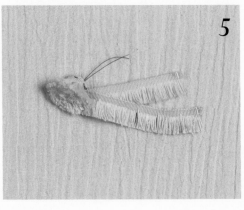

5. Place the green strip on top of the yellow strip and roll up, tacking the remaining selvedges as you go. Position the rolled-up fringe in the center of the flower and tack to the flower and buckram. Trim the buckram close to the stitching in back.

Grow a field of daisies on the side of a bright red straw hat. Mount your daisies on stem wires and mix them with a bunch of live red tulips. Or, display a daisy on the center front of a navy-blue baseball cap!

Pansy

Viola

Pansy is one of the many members in the viola family. The self-seeding plant prefers moist, humus-rich soil and full to partial shade. Pansy comes from the French "pensée" (a thought or remembrance) and is associated with "easing of the heart," hence its other name, "heartsease."

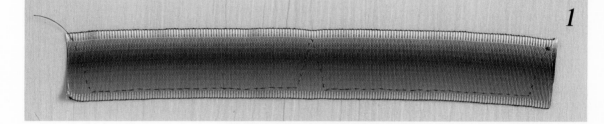

1

1a

MATERIALS

- 30" of 1⅝"-wide green/fuchsia shaded grosgrain

- 3" square of buckram

- 2" of ⅝"-wide yellow grosgrain

- 16" of 1"-wide green wire-edge taffeta

1 and 1a. Cut a 12" piece of the shaded ribbon. Starting ¼" from one cut end, sew gathering stitches along the fuchsia edge of the ribbon as shown in photo above. Pull up the thread tightly; knot. Overlap the two sections of the ribbon about 1" in the center to resemble the top petals of a pansy. Sew the gathered edge of the petals to the center of the 3" square of buckram.

 For a pleated pansy, double the measurements in any width. Crimp the ribbon with a Pullen pleater, making sure to first pull the wires from the selvedges.

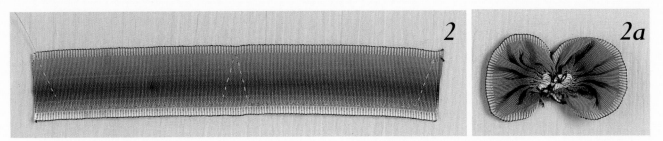

2 and 2a. Cut a 10" piece of shaded ribbon. Sew gathering stitches along the green edge of the the ribbon as shown in the photo above. Pull up the thread tightly; knot. Shape the petals to resemble a butterfly.

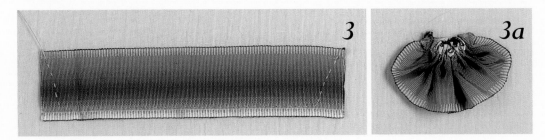

3 and 3a. Cut a 7½" piece of shaded ribbon. Sew gathering stitches along the green edge of the ribbon as shown in the photo above. Shape into a single petal.

4. Place the butterfly-shape petals on top of the overlapping petals so the centers match. Place the single petal at the base of the other petals and sew to the center.

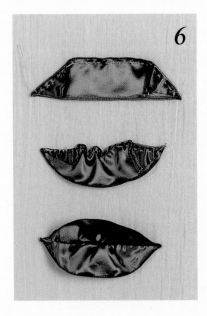

5. Cut one selvedge from the 2" piece of yellow grosgrain. Pull out several threads and tie them together at the center. Sew to the center of the flower.

6. Cut two 8" pieces of green taffeta. Fold each piece in half widthwise, then fold down the corners as shown in the photo above. With double thread, sew a small running stitch up the diagonal edge with the cut end, along the top edge and down the opposite diagonal edge. Pull up the thread slightly, but do not finish it off. Open the layers and arrange the gathers carefully, keeping most of them in the center and toward the bottom of the leaf. Secure the thread with three to four stitches in the seam. Sew the leaves to the buckram behind the flower. Trim the buckram.

Vintage Rose

The Vintage Rose is one of my favorite fantasy flowers. It's based on the antique peony-like roses, which, when dried, take on a lovely crinkled look. These are easy to make and add a great deal of charm to a hat or picture frame.

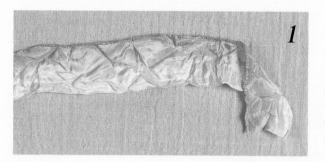

1. Hold the 1⅓-yard length of ribbon under warm water; crunch it up into a tight ball in your hands and squeeze as much water out as possible; then leave it in this tight wad to dry.

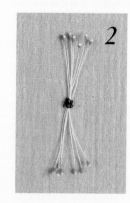

2. Secure a small bundle of stamens in the center by wrapping with thread.

MATERIALS

- 1⅓ yards of 1"-wide pink shaded wire-edge taffeta

- 7" of 1"-wide green wire-edge taffeta for one leaf

- Stamens

- 4" square of buckram

- 3" square of felt

- Pin back

3. When the ribbon is dry, unroll it. Fold down the right-hand end as shown so about 1" hangs below to form a "handle." Fold the stamens in half and stitch them to the folded portion of the ribbon.

4. Wrap the right-hand end of the ribbon loosely around the stamens to form the center bud. Stitch carefully through the stamens and lower selvedge.

5. Sew the center bud through the lower selvedge onto the buckram.

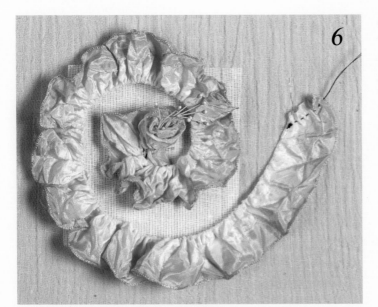

6. Find the end of the wire at the left-hand end of the lower selvedge. Pull the wire up to about 11". Securing it from underneath, gently wind the gathered ribbon around the bud in the same direction as you rolled the center, allowing a ¼" space between the gathered rows until it resembles a full-blown rose.

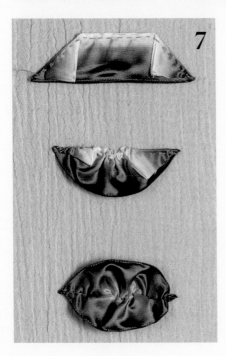

7. Fold the 7" piece of green taffeta in half widthwise, then fold down the corners as shown in the photo at left. With double thread, sew a small running stitch up the diagonal edge with the cut end, along the top edge and down the opposite diagonal edge. Pull up the thread slightly, but do not knot it. Open the layers and arrange the gathers carefully, keeping most of them in the center and toward the bottom of the leaf. Secure the thread with three to four stitches in the seam. Sew leaf to buckram behind flower. Trim the buckram to a round or oval shape, making sure no buckram is visible in front. Cut a felt circle or oval slightly larger than the buckram. Sew a pin back to the felt, centering it near the top. Sew or glue the felt circle to the buckram.

Turk's-cap Lily

Lilium superbum

One of the many species of the Lilium, Turk's cap is found in wet woods and meadows in the Southeast corner of the United States. It blooms from July through September. The Turk's-cap lily is similar to the tiger lily but greater in height.

MATERIALS

- 1⅓ yards of 1"-wide orange wire-edge taffeta or grosgrain

- One large and six small stamens

- 2" of 1- or 1½"-wide green wire-edge taffeta for casing

- 8" of 1"-wide green shaded wire-edge taffeta or grosgrain for leaf

- Green stem wire

- Green floral tape or ⅝"-wide green ribbon

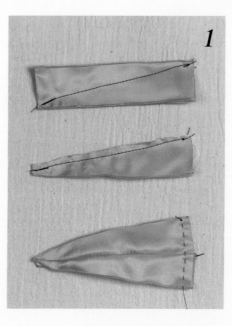

1. Cut orange ribbon into six 8" pieces. Fold each piece in half widthwise. Using small running or machine stitches and beginning at the cut end, sew diagonally to the opposite folded end. Trim the folded side of the ribbon to within ⅛" of the seam. Apply clear nail polish to the edges of the seam allowance to prevent fraying.

2. Paint the large stamen brown. Tie the six small stamens and the one large stamen together by wrapping the center of the bundle with thread.

3. Use a running stitch to join all six petals about ¼" above the straight ends. Join the last petal to the first one. Draw up the thread and insert the stamens in the center of the flower; pull the thread tight and wrap it several times around the base of the flower, to create a stub.

4. Remove wire from both selvedges of the 2" piece of green taffeta. Finger-press a ¼" fold in one end. Beginning with the cut end, loosely wrap the ribbon around the stub of the flower and secure along the top selvedge. Neatly sew the folded end in place. Knot and clip the thread.

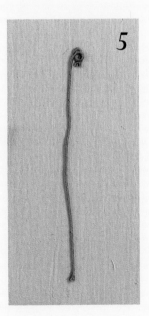

5. Sew running stitches along the lower selvedge of the casing. Make a loop in one end of the stem wire and insert the loop in the casing. Pull up the thread to gather the casing around the stem wire. Knot and clip the thread.

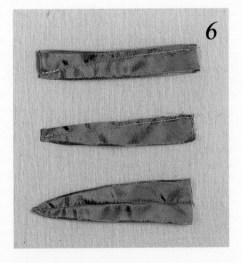

6. The leaf is made the same way as the petals. Starting at the base of the flower, wrap the stem with floral tape or ⅝"-wide green ribbon for about 2". Pinch or pleat the bottom of the leaf around the stem wire, secure with tape or ribbon, and continue to wrap the rest of the stem.

When finished, add a few purple spots to the inner portion of each lily petal for a more authentic representation.

Cabochon Rose

Another example of one of my creative fantasy flowers, the cabochon rose works up quickly and easily. Petals need not be made—a simple gathering of the ribbon forms the flower. For spectacular results, try this versatile bloom in a variety of ribbon widths and colors.

MATERIALS

- 1½ yards of 1"-wide pink wire-edge taffeta for flower

- 4" of 1"-wide pink wire-edge taffeta for rosebud

- 7" of 1"-wide green wire-edge taffeta for leaf

- 3" square of buckram

- 3" square of felt

- Pin back

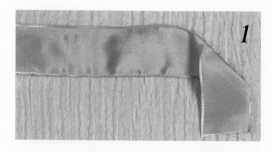

1. Fold down about 2" on the right-hand end of the ribbon for the flower as shown so that 1" hangs below to form a "handle."

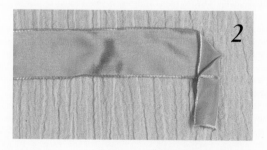

2. Fold the outermost half of the handle over onto the other half. This will become the center of the rose.

3. Now roll the handle from right to left, coiling the ribbon loosely to make the rolled center of the rose.

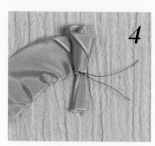

4. When you have coiled two or three turns, and the top is a perfect circle, fold the top selvedge back to form a gentle bias fold, which will become the edge of a rose petal. Roll the rose to the left, so that the bias fold becomes part of the center. Hold the "handle" in your right hand as you roll; this will keep the rose loosely rolled. Secure the ribbon at the base of the rose with a few stitches. Repeat this rolling and folding step once more, stitching to secure.

5. Sew the center bud through the lower selvedge onto the buckram.

6. Find the end of the wire at the left-hand end of the lower selvedge. Push the ribbon down onto the wire, gathering the ribbon to about 11". Cut the protruding wire, leaving a short end. Bend the short end back and secure with thread. Securing the gathered ribbon from underneath, gently wind it around the bud in the same direction as you rolled the center, allowing a ¼" space between the gathered rows until it resembles a full-blown rose. When it is firmly attached to the buckram, trim the buckram close to the stitching.

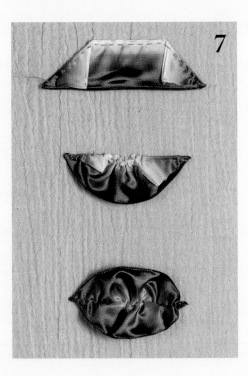

7. Fold the 7" piece of green taffeta in half widthwise, then fold down the corners as shown in the photo at left. With double thread, sew a small running stitch up the diagonal edge cut the raw end, along the top edge, and down the opposite diagonal edge. Pull up the thread slightly, but do not knot it. Open the layers and arrange the gathers carefully, keeping most of them in the center and toward the bottom of the leaf. Secure the thread with three to four stitches in the seam. Set the leaf aside.

Following Steps 1–5, use the 4" piece of pink ribbon to make a rosebud. Angle the end toward the "handle" and stitch closed. Sew the leaf and rosebud to the buckram behind the flower. Trim the buckram to a round or oval shape, making sure no buckram is visible in front. Cut a felt circle or oval slightly larger than the buckram. Sew a pin back to the felt, centering it near the top. Sew or glue the felt piece to the buckram.

Cosmos

Cosmos

Several species are native to the American Southwest; the annual Cosmos bipinnatus is popular in the flower garden. Most cosmos flower rather late in the season and are best on light, sandy soils in regions with long growing seasons.

MATERIALS

- 16" of 1"-wide pink shaded wire-edge taffeta

- 6" of ⅝"-wide yellow grosgrain

- 1½" square of buckram

- 1"x8" strip of fusible webbing

1. Remove wires from pink taffeta and fold ribbon in half widthwise. Insert webbing between layers of folded ribbon, removing paper backing first. Cover ribbon with a cotton cloth and fuse, following manufacturer's instructions. From fused ribbon, cut eight 1" pieces. Use a pinking shears to shape the top as shown.

2. Join the petals with running stitches about ⅛" above the straight bottom edges. Connect the first petal to the last petal.

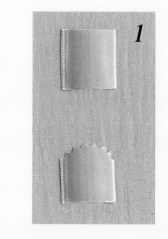

3. Pull the thread tightly to close the center of the flower; knot and clip the thread. Sew the flower to the buckram square.

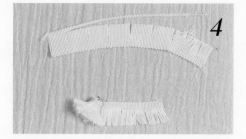

4. Cut top selvedge from yellow grosgrain. Make several perpendicular cuts to within ¼" of bottom selvedge. Use a pin or an awl to pull out threads, creating a fringe. Roll up the strip, tacking the selvedge as you go. Tack the rolled-up fringe to the center of the flower and the buckram. Trim the buckram in back.

Coreopsis

Coreopsis lanceolata

The eight yellow ray petals of the coreopsis bloom are often notched or toothed at their tips. You can spot them in dry fields and prairies, where they bloom from May through August.

MATERIALS

- 16" of ⅝"-wide yellow wire-edge taffeta
- 2½" of ⅝"-wide gold grosgrain
- 2½" of ⅝"-wide brown grosgrain
- 1½" square of buckram

1. Remove wires from edges of yellow taffeta and cut the ribbon into eight 2" pieces. Fold each piece in half widthwise; trim the cut edges with pinking shears to a rounded edge.

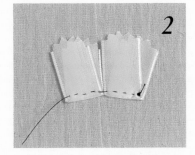

2. Using running stitches, join the petals along their folded edges, offsetting the layers of each petal slightly.

3. Sew the first petal to the last petal. Pull up the thread tightly and close the center. Sew the flower to the buckram square.

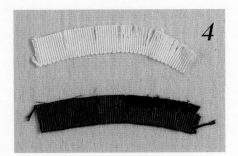

4. Trim each piece of grosgrain to ⅜" wide by cutting off one selvedge. Every ½", make a perpendicular cut to within ⅛" of the selvedge. Using a pin or an awl, pull out the threads to create a fringed strip.

5. Place the brown strip on top of the gold strip and roll up, using thread to tack the selvedges together as you go. Position the rolled-up fringe in the center of the flower and tack to the flower and buckram. Trim the buckram close to the stitching in back.

Sunflower

Helianthus annuus

Always drawing happy smiles from passersby, the sunflower blooms in fields and prairies from June through October. The seeds in the center of the large sunny flowerheads provide food for birds and oil for human consumption.

MATERIALS

- 2 yards of 1"-wide yellow/gold wire-edge taffeta for flower

- 20" of 1½"-wide green wire-edge taffeta for leaves

- 7" of ⅝"-wide dark brown grosgrain

- 2" of ⅝"-wide yellow grosgrain

- 7" of ⅝"-wide black grosgrain

- 3" square of buckram

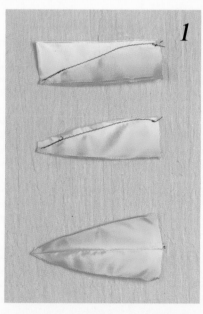

1. Cut eleven 6" pieces of yellow/gold taffeta. Fold each piece in half width-wise, with all gold shading at the bottom. Using small running stitches or machine straight stitches and beginning at the cut end, sew diagonally to the opposite folded end. Secure thread with a backstitch; clip thread. Trim ribbon to ⅛" from seam. Seal cut edges with clear nail polish to prevent fraying. Open ribbons up into petals.

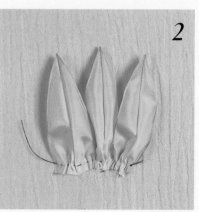

2. Join all eleven petals with running stitches about ¼" above the straight bottom edges. Connect the first petal to the last petal.

3

3. Pull the thread tightly to close the center of the flower; knot and clip thread. Arrange the petals. Sew the flower to the buckram square.

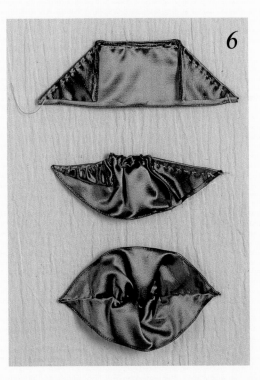

6

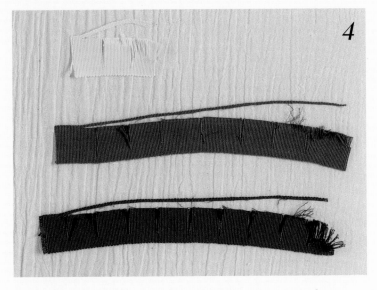

4

4. Cut top selvedge from each piece of grosgrain. In each piece, make perpendicular cuts at 1" intervals to within ¼" of the lower selvedge. Do not cut completely through ribbon. Using a needle or awl, fray the ribbon to the ¼" level on all three pieces.

6. Cut two 10" pieces of green taffeta. Fold each piece in half widthwise, then fold down the corners as shown in the photo above. With double thread, sew a small running stitch up the diagonal edge with the cut end, along the top edge, and down the opposite diagonal edge. Pull up the thread slightly, but do not knot it. Open the layers and arrange the gathers carefully, keeping most of them in the center and toward the bottom of the leaf. When you are happy with the leaf's shape, secure the thread with three to four stitches in the seam. Sew the second ribbon in the same way. Sew leaves to buckram behind flower. Trim the buckram to a round or oval shape, making sure no buckram is visible in front.

5

5. Place the brown strip on top of the black strip and the yellow strip on top of the brown strip, matching their left-hand edges. Beginning at the left end, roll up the strips, using brown thread to tack the selvedges together as you go. Position the rolled-up fringe in the center of the flower and tack to flower and buckram.

Johnny Jump-up

Viola tricolor

Johnny jump-ups are usually found in groups, in a wide variety of habitats varying from wet to dry and from woodland to prairie. They typically bloom from April through June— sometimes all summer.

1. Fold the 5" piece of purple shaded taffeta in half and make a crease; unfold. Beginning $\frac{1}{8}$" from one end and using a double thread, sew running stitches diagonally to the lower selvedge. Sew along the bottom selvedge to $\frac{1}{4}$" before the crease and angle the stitches upward to the crease at the top selvedge. Carry a stitch over top crease and angle back down to the lower edge. Stitch along the lower selvedge to $\frac{1}{4}$" from the end and angle up to the top selvedge $\frac{1}{8}$" from the end. Pull thread tight to gather ribbon; backstitch and knot thread. Sew the gathers to the top half of the buckram square.

MATERIALS

- 5" of $\frac{5}{8}$"-wide purple shaded wire-edge taffeta

- $4\frac{1}{2}$" of $\frac{5}{8}$"-wide lavender moiré taffeta

- $2\frac{1}{2}$" of $\frac{5}{8}$"-wide yellow shaded wire-edge taffeta

- $1\frac{1}{2}$" of $\frac{5}{8}$"-wide black grosgrain

- 2" square of buckram

- Green stem wire

2. Fold the 4½" piece of lavender moiré taffeta in half and make a crease; unfold. Beginning ⅛" from one end and using a double thread, sew running stitches diagonally to the bottom selvedge. Sew along the bottom selvedge to ¼" before the crease and angle the stitches upward to the crease at the top selvedge. Carry a stitch over top crease and angle back down to the lower edge. Stitch along the lower selvedge to ¼" from the end and angle up to the top selvedge ⅛" from the end. Pull thread tight to gather ribbon; backstitch and knot thread. Sew gathers to buckram square slightly below purple gathers.

3. Beginning ⅛" from the lighter selvedge and using a double thread, sew running stitches diagonally to the darker selvedge. Sew along the darker selvedge to ¼" before the end and angle the stitches downward to the lighter selvedge. Pull thread tight to gather ribbon; backstitch and knot thread. Sew to gathers of lavender ribbon, stitching through buckram at same time. Trim the buckram close to the stitching in back.

5. To use this flower in a bouquet, make a tight loop at one end of an 8" piece of stem wire and sew the loop to the back of the flower.

4. Cut one selvedge from the 1½" piece of black grosgrain. Pull out 8 to 10 threads and wrap the threads together at the center with matching thread. Sew to the center of the flower.

Lupine

Lupinus perennis

Most species are found in the southwestern states and on the Pacific Coast and bloom from April through July. One very famous lupine, the Texas Bluebonnet, is the state flower of Texas.

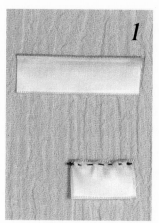

1. There are 15 flowers and 12 buds on each lupine stem. Each flower consists of three buds, so you need to make a total of 57 buds. Cut the taffeta for the flowers into 2" pieces. Remove the wires. Fold each piece in half width-wise and sew together along one selvedge. Turn seam to the inside. When making flowers, position the darker shading at the top for the center bud and the lighter shading at the top for the two outer buds.

2. Beginning at the seam, sew small running stitches along one end to the open selvedge, then along the open selvedge, then along the other end, ending up at the seam again. Pull thread to gather petal. Knot the thread but do not clip.

MATERIALS

- 3½ yards of ⅝"-wide blue or purple wire-edge taffeta for flowers and buds

- 1½ yards of ⅝"-wide green wire-edge taffeta for casings

- 1" piece of 1"-wide yellow grosgrain

- 7" of ⅝"-wide green wire-edge taffeta for one leaf

- Green stem wire

- Green floral tape

3. Sew three buds together through the gathers. Position the middle bud upward and point the other two toward the back. Join the two outer buds at the back with slip stitches.

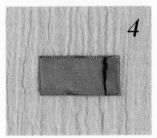

4. Cut twenty-seven 1½" pieces of green taffeta. Remove wires. Finger-press a ¼" fold in one end of each piece.

5. Beginning with the cut end, wrap the ribbon around the stub of the flower or the bottom of the bud and secure along the top selvedge.

6. Neatly sew the folded end in place. Knot and clip the thread.

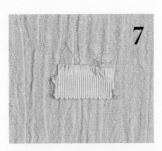

7. Cut one selvedge from the yellow grosgrain. Pull out a few threads. Fold the threads in half and glue into the center of a flower. Trim so the threads barely show. Repeat for some of the other flowers.

8. Sew the flowers to the stem in rows of three or four, beginning about 7" to 8" from the top of a long stem wire. All stitching is done at the bottom of the casing, with the casing sewn closed at the same time. Add the next row about 1" above the first. When you've used all of the flowers, add the buds between the flowers in a similar staggered fashion.

9. Fold the green ribbon in half widthwise. Place the stem wire diagonally along the length of the ribbon. Machine zigzag stitch over the wire, from the left top corner down to the right bottom corner. Open up the leaf. Pinch the bottom raw edges together and wrap with floral tape. Using floral tape, attach the leaf stem to the flower stem.

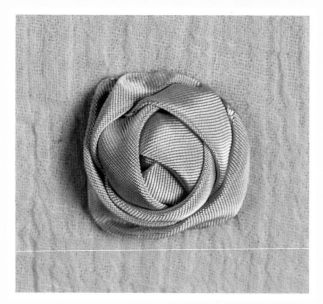

Chou Rose

Rosa centifolia

The chou or "cabbage" rose is a recurring star in the gorgeous flower paintings of the Dutch Old Masters. The name "cabbage" stems from the time when vegetable growers added cut flowers to their wares to enhance their market assortment.

MATERIALS

- 27" of 1"-wide ribbon

- 3" square of buckram

For all bouquet flowers, make a loop in the end of a #20 gauge green cloth-covered stem wire (about 7" total). Sew the loop to the finished back of the flower.

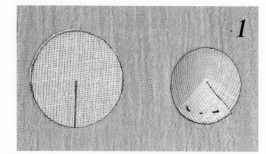

1. Cut a 2½"-diameter circle from the buckram, and carefully slash from the edge to the center. Overlap the cut edges about 1" and stitch together along the edge, forming a cone shape.

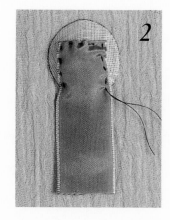

2. Turn under ¼" at one end of the ribbon and place over the top of the cone. Using a knotted double thread, secure the ribbon to the buckram along the folded end and along the side edges with small running stitches. Let the needle and thread dangle in readiness for the next stitches.

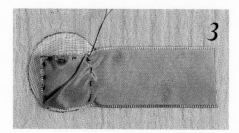

3. Swing the ribbon counterclockwise a quarter turn, creating a diagonal fold on top of the cone. Stitch across the width of the ribbon from the lower right corner to the upper right corner.

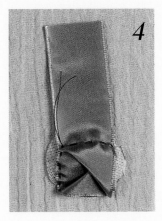

4. Swing the ribbon counterclockwise another quarter turn, again creating a diagonal fold on top of the cone. Stitch across the width of the ribbon from the upper right corner to the upper left corner.

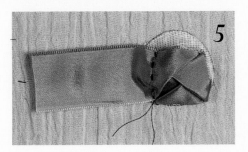

5. Make a third quarter turn and stitch across the width again, gradually curving your line of stitches to follow the natural curve of the cone.

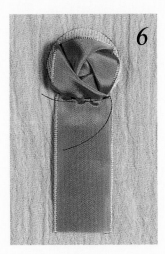

6. Make another quarter turn and secure the ribbon across the width to the buckram. A small "window" should become visible in the center of the cone.

8. When the cone is completely covered with folds, trim the remaining length of ribbon and secure the end to the back of the buckram.

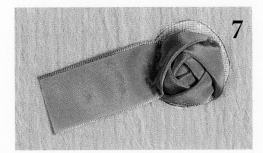

7. Position your subsequent folds just enough below the previous folds so the folds are not covered up— they form the petals of the rose.

Wild Poppy

Eschscholzia

Bright flowers that burst open at the first touch of sunlight—these are the poppies that surrounded Dorothy on her trek to the Emerald City. Found in grasslands, meadows, and dunes, they bloom from February through September.

1

2

3

MATERIALS

- 24" of 1½"-wide or 20" of 1"-wide wire-edge red shaded taffeta

- 1½" of ⅝"-wide black grosgrain

- 3" square of buckram

To give a distinctive wrinkled, paper-thin quality to the poppy, soak the ribbon in hot water for 2 minutes. Wring out excess water. Roll the ribbon into a tight ball; air-dry.

1. Remove the wire from the light-shaded edge of the taffeta. Fold it in half widthwise and make a crease; fold in half again and make another crease; unfold. Beginning at one dark-shaded end, sew running stitches diagonally to the lower selvedge. Sew along the lower selvedge to ¼" before the crease. Angle the stitches upward, carry a stitch over the crease at the top, and begin to angle back down to the lower selvedge. Stitch along the lower selvedge and angle stitches back up; you've completed two sections. Repeat across the ribbon.

2. Pull up gathers; backstitch and knot. Sew gathers to center of buckram square.

3. Cut one selvedge from black grosgrain. Pull out two bunches of threads. Stitch in crisscross fashion to center of flower. Trim the buckram close to the stitching on the back.

Wild Rose

Rosa

Many species of wild roses line our country lanes and bloom in open woodlands. Common names such as meadow rose and sweet briar change from state to state. Besides their decorative value, the fruits or "hips" of the rose are rich in vitamin C.

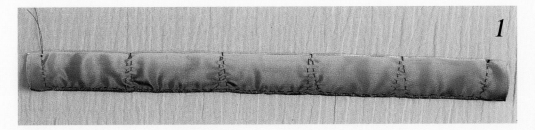

1. Starting ⅜" from one end, mark coral selvedge at 2¼" intervals. Using double thread, sew gathering stitches along the edges of the ribbon as shown in the photo at left, carrying the thread around the selvedge at each mark.

MATERIALS

- 12" of 1"-wide coral/green wire-edge taffeta
- Stamens
- 2" square of buckram

2. Pull up the thread to form the petals. Sew the first petal to the last, leaving a ¼" center; knot thread. Sew the flower to a buckram square.

3. Wrap thread around the center of a bunch of stamens.

4. Fold stamens in half and sew to the center of the flower, stitching through the buckram. Trim the buckram close to the stitching on the back.

Black-eyed Susan

Rudbeckia hirta

An ideal plant for wildflower meadows, the black-eyed Susan, also known as Autumn Sun, reseeds well and flowers particularly well during long, hot summers. The plants are found in fields, prairies, open woods, and waste places and bloom from June through October.

MATERIALS

- 3⅓ yards of 1"-wide yellow/gold shaded wire-edge taffeta

- 3" square of buckram

- 11" of ½"-wide black velvet tubing

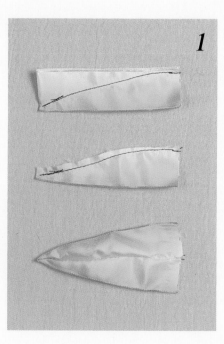

1. Cut seventeen 7" pieces of yellow/gold taffeta. Fold each piece in half widthwise, with either all dark shading or all light shading at the top. Using small running stitches or machine straight stitches and beginning at the cut end, sew diagonally to the folded end as shown in photo. Backstitch for ½"; knot and clip thread. Trim seam allowance close to stitching and seal the cut edges with clear nail polish to prevent fraying. Open ribbons into petals.

2. Use a running stitch to join the seventeen petals ¼" from the cut edges.

3. Pull the thread tight to gather the petals. Connect the first petal to the last petal. Pull the thread tight to close the center of the flower; knot and clip thread. Arrange the petals. Sew the flower to the buckram square.

To make a smaller version of this 17-petal black-eyed Susan, you'll need 2½ yards of ⅝"-wide yellow/gold wired taffeta. Cut the ribbon into 17 five-inch pieces. Fold each piece in half and make in the same way as the large one. Use 6" of tubing for the flower center.

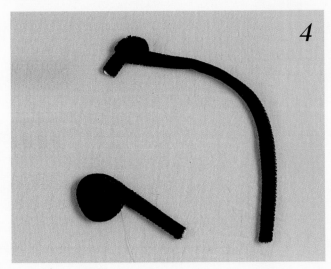

4. Make a double knot in one end of the black velvet tubing. Sew the knot to the center of the flower and buckram. Coil the remaining tubing around and on top of the knot, tacking it in place as you form a raised ½" dome shape. Trim the buckram close to the stitching in back of the flower.

Purple Coneflower

Echinacea purpurea

The large daisy-like flower head of the purple coneflower sits firmly on its thick stem. The vigorous flowers appear in summer and continue blooming for two months or more.

MATERIALS

- 1¼ yards of 1"-wide dark pink shaded wire-edge taffeta for flower

- 16" of 1"-wide green/pink shaded wire-edge taffeta for leaves

- 4½" of ⅝"-wide brown grosgrain

- 4½" of ⅝"-wide burgundy grosgrain

- 3" square of buckram

1. Cut eleven 4" pieces of dark pink taffeta. Fold each piece in half widthwise, with the dark shading at the bottom. Using small running stitches or machine straight stitches and beginning at the cut end, sew diagonally to the opposite folded end as shown in photo at left. Backstitch for ½"; knot and clip thread. Trim the seam allowance close to the stitching and seal the cut edges with clear nail polish to prevent fraying. Open up the ribbons into petals.

2. Use a running stitch to join the eleven petals ¼" from the cut edges.

For all bouquet flowers, make a loop in the end of a #20 gauge green cloth-covered stem wire (about 7" total). Sew the loop to the finished back of the flower.

3. Pull the thread tight to gather the leaves and connect the first petal to the last petal. Pull the thread tight to close the center of the flower; knot and clip thread. Sew the flower to the buckram square.

4. Cut top selvedge from each piece of grosgrain. In each piece, make six perpendicular cuts at equal intervals to within ¼" of the bottom selvedge. Do not cut completely through ribbon. Using a heavy pin or an awl, fray the ribbon down to the ¼" level on both pieces.

5. Place the burgundy strip on top of the brown strip. Beginning at the left end, roll up strips, using brown thread to tack the selvedges together as you go. Position the rolled-up fringe in the center of the flower and tack to the flower and buckram.

6. Cut two 8" pieces of green taffeta. Fold each piece in half widthwise, then fold down the corners as shown in the photo at left. With double thread, sew a small running stitch up the diagonal edge with the cut end, along the top edge and down the opposite diagonal edge. Pull up the thread slightly, but do not knot it. Open the layers and arrange the gathers carefully, keeping most of them in the center and toward the bottom of the leaf. Secure the thread with three to four stitches in the seam. Sew the second leaf in the same way. Sew the leaves to the buckram behind the flower. Trim the buckram to a round or oval shape, making sure it is not visible in front.

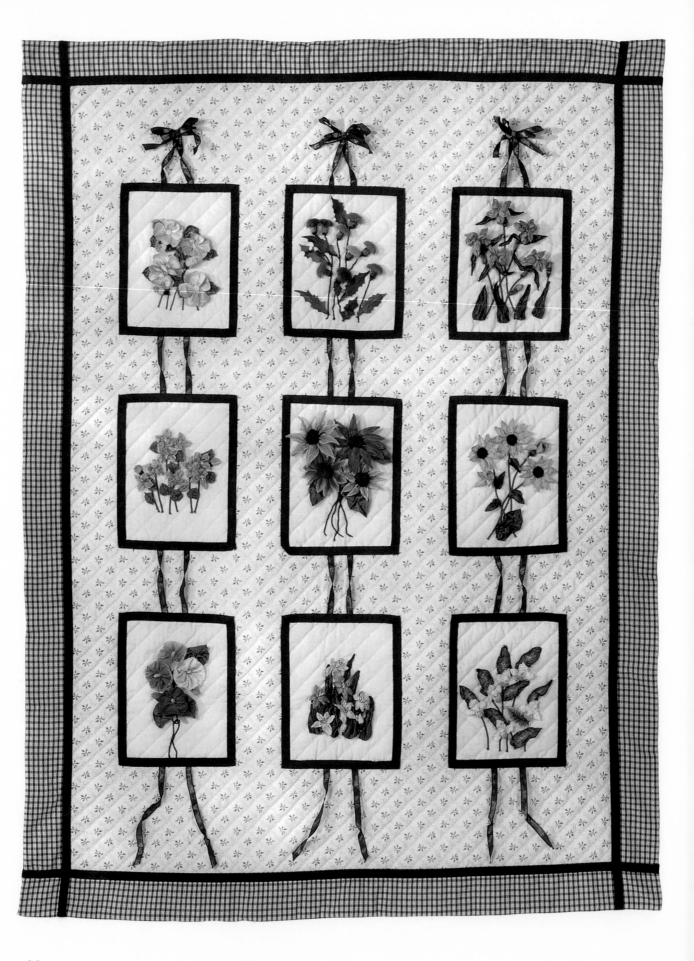

Cam's Wildflower Quilt

Finding new applications for creative output challenges every artist. I embrace this delightful challenge wholeheartedly and always develop new and surprising ways for showcasing my unique flowers. To display my wildflowers, I not only fabricate faux bouquets and blooms for hats, boxes, and picture frames, I even work my lifelike florals into quilts. I encourage everyone reading this book to invent their own uses for their floral artworks; however, the quilt was so much fun to make, I just have to share it with you.

You'll find, when making projects from this book, that ribbonry is a wonderfully accessible art form. I am not a trained seamstress, nor do I follow conventional sewing rules; rather, I believe in free interpretation. All you need are a few simple tools, a little patience, and imagination.

What you need:
- 3 yards of gingham fabric for the back
- 1½ yards of floral fabric for the front
- ⅔ yard of muslin for the flower blocks
- 11 yards of 1"-wide grosgrain ribbon for the block borders
- 6 yards of 1"-wide grosgrain ribbon for the quilt's inner border
- 4½ yards of ⅝"-wide grosgrain ribbon for the block "picture hangers"
- Batting
- Ribbons and materials to complete the nine wildflower blocks as described on pages 100–117 (available as kits from The Ribbonry, see Sources on page 140)

Quilt the layers first:
Cut a 1-yard piece of the gingham fabric into two 36" x 22" pieces. Sew the pieces together along the 22" edges. Sew this piece to the side edge of the remaining 2-yard piece. Place the gingham fabric with the right side down on a table. Place the batting on top. Center the floral fabric onto the batting and pin the layers together. Make nine wildflower blocks as described on pages 100–117. Referring to the photo for placement, baste the blocks in place. Hand- or machine-quilt a diagonal pattern with 1½" spaces across the quilt, being careful not to catch any flowers, leaves, or stems in the quilting stitches.

Bind the edges:
Cut the excess batting, leaving a 4" margin all around the floral fabric. Cut the excess gingham fabric, leaving an 8" margin all around the floral fabric. Fold the gingham fabric over to the right side of the quilt so the raw edges of the fabrics meet. Referring to the photo opposite, cover the raw edges with the grosgrain ribbon.

Finish the quilt:
Measure and cut the ⅝"-wide ribbon pieces for the "picture hangers"; tack the pieces in place. Frame the blocks with 1"-wide grosgrain ribbon, covering the raw edges.

Virginia Rose

Rosa virginiana

The Virginia rose is found from southern Ontario to Nova Scotia, and south to Virginia and North Carolina, west to Alabama, Tennessee, and Missouri. The rose hips are edible and rich in vitamin C. This flower's beautiful autumnal foliage is a unique feature.

MATERIALS

- 3 yards of 1"-wide pink shaded wire-edge taffeta

- 2¼ yards of 1"-wide green wire-edge taffeta for leaves and casings

- Five 3" squares of buckram

- 1¼ yards of moss-green cording for stems

- 30" of ⅛"-wide yellow grosgrain

- 2" piece of 1"-wide yellow grosgrain

- 8" x 10" piece of natural muslin

- Small amount of stuffing

- Fusible webbing

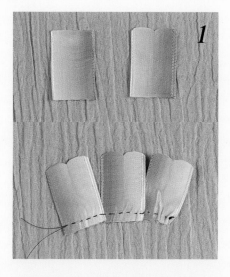

2. Cut two 1" pieces from 1"-wide yellow grosgrain. Cut one selvedge from each 1" piece and pull out several threads. Sew two collections of strands in an X pattern to the center of each flower.

1. Cut thirty 3" pieces of pink shaded ribbon. Remove wires. Fold each piece in half widthwise. Cut six 1½" x 1" pieces of fusible webbing. Remove paper backing. Insert each piece between the layers of a folded ribbon. Cover ribbons with a cotton cloth and fuse, following webbing manufacturer's instructions. Fold each petal in half lengthwise and cut the top edge in a rounded shape; unfold. Using running stitches, join six petals ¼" from the straight edges. Pull the thread to gather tightly, then join the ends; knot thread. Sew the rose to the center of a buckram square. Make five flowers.

3. Cut five 6" pieces of ⅛"-wide yellow grosgrain. Sew tiny running stitches through the center of each piece.

4. Pull thread on ⅛"-wide grosgrain as tight as possible to gather ribbon. Sew to flower center in a circular shape, stitching through the buckram. Trim the buckram ¼" from stitching.

5. Cut three 4" pieces of pink shaded ribbon. Remove wires. Fold each piece in half widthwise and sew a seam ¼" from cut ends. Turn seam to inside. Sew running stitches around the perimeter, ¼" below the top selvedge. Pull the thread tightly to gather; knot thread. Place a small amount of stuffing inside. Sew running stitches closely around bottom selvedge. Pull the thread tightly to gather; knot thread.

6. Cut three 2" pieces of green taffeta. Remove wires. Wrap ribbon around the bottom of a rose pod, overlapping the ends. Turn top cut end under ¼" and stitch the top selvedge to the bottom of the pod. Blind-stitch the side seam; knot thread. Sew running stitches along the lower selvedge and insert one end of a 5" length of green cording. Pull the thread tightly around cording; backstitch and knot thread.

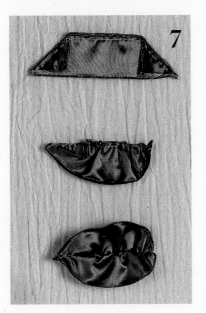

7. Cut ten 7" pieces of green taffeta. Fold each piece in half widthwise. Fold down top corners and, beginning at the cut end, sew with a running stitch as shown in the photo. Pull up thread to gather fabric and open layers to reveal a leaf. Adjust gathers towards base to create a pear shape; knot thread. Cut a 5" piece of cording for each flower stem. Apply clear nail polish to ends to prevent fraying. Arrange pieces on muslin as shown in drawing at right or as desired; stitch in place.

Virginia Rose

Canada Thistle

Cirsium arvense

This fragrant small flower blooms in fields and pastures all over North America from June through August. It originated in Europe and was introduced by way of Canada.

MATERIALS

- 24" of 1"-wide dark pink grosgrain

- 8" of 1"-wide light pink grosgrain

- 8" of 1"-wide lavender grosgrain

- 24" of 1"-wide purple grosgrain

- 1½ yards of 1"-wide moss-green taffeta for leaves and casings

- 1 yard of green soutache braid

- Fusible webbing

- 8" x 10" piece of natural muslin

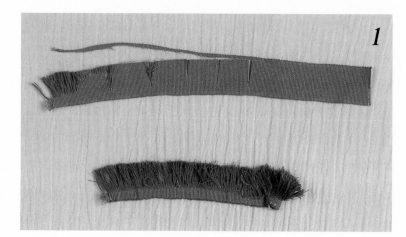

1. Cut an 8" piece of 1"-wide grosgrain. Cut off top selvedge. Space seven ¾"-deep clips 1" apart. Use a thick pin or an awl to fray the piece by pulling threads out to about ¼" from bottom selvedge. Tightly coil or roll up the frayed ribbon, stitching and securing the coil at bottom selvedge as you roll. Create eight flowers, using dark pink, light pink, lavender, and purple grosgrain. For a more natural appearance, cut some ribbons 6" or 7" long.

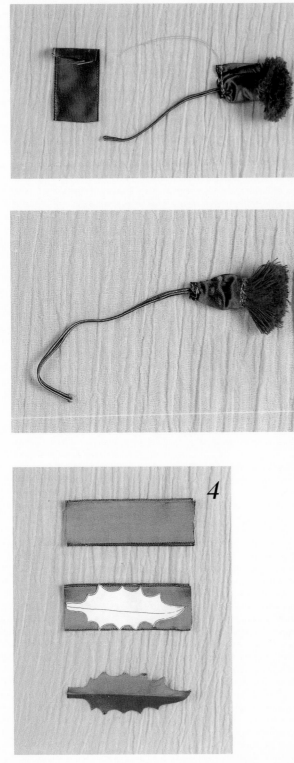

2. Cut eight 2" pieces of green taffeta. Remove wires. Wrap ribbon around the bottom of the unfrayed edge of a pink or purple bloom, overlapping the ends. Turn top cut end under ¼" and stitch the top selvedge to the bottom of the bloom.

3. Blind-stitch the side seam; knot thread. Sew running stitches along the bottom selvedge of casing. For stem, insert one end of a length of green braid; vary the length of each stem as shown in drawing below to fit the muslin. Pull the thread tightly around the braid; backstitch, and knot thread. Seal end of braid with clear nail polish.

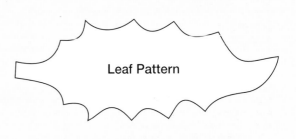

Leaf Pattern

5. Arrange pieces on muslin as shown in drawing below or as desired. Stitch in place.

4. Cut six 6" pieces of green taffeta. Fold each piece in half widthwise. Cut six 3" x 1" pieces of fusible webbing. Remove paper backing. Insert each piece between layers of a folded ribbon. Cover ribbons with a cotton cloth and fuse, following webbing manufacturer's instructions. Trace and cut out a paper leaf pattern. Trace leaf pattern onto each folded ribbon; cut out. Fold each leaf in half and finger-press to make a vein.

Thistle

Blue Flag Iris

Iridaceae versicolor

Grows on fertile soils that are well drained, and blooms from May to July. The Iris inspired the "fleur de lys" insignia of the royal family of France. The dried root, called orris root, contains an oil that has been used in perfume since ancient times.

MATERIALS

- 3½ yards of ⅝"-wide blue wire-edge taffeta

- 3½ yards of ⅝"-wide green wire-edge taffeta for leaves and casings

- 3" piece of 1"-wide yellow grosgrain

- 1 yard of green soutache braid

- 20" of green stem wire

- Green floral tape

- 8" x 10" piece of natural muslin

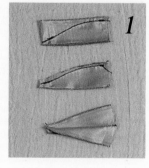

1. There are three small and three large petals in each iris. For five flowers, cut fifteen 3" and fifteen 4" pieces of blue taffeta. Set aside the 4" pieces. Fold each 3" piece in half widthwise. Using a straight stitch, machine-sew from top corner of cut end to bottom corner of folded end. Backstitch and clip thread. Trim ribbon to ⅛" from seam. Seal raw edges with clear nail polish to prevent raveling. Open ribbon up to a small triangular shaped petal.

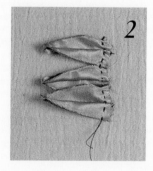

2. Using running stitches, join three petals ¼" from the straight edges. Pull the thread to gather tightly, then join the ends; knot the thread.

3. Cut five 4" pieces of green stem wire. Bend one end of wire to form a hook. Insert straight end through center of three petals. Wrap thread around the petal ends several times; knot thread. Set aside.

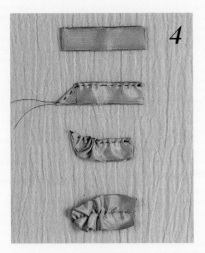

4

5

5. Using running stitches, join three petals ¼" from the straight edges. Pull thread to gather, and join the ends. Do not pull the tread too tight.

6

6. Insert the wire end of a set of 3" petals. Stitch both sets of three together at the stem and tightly wrap with 2" of floral tape, stretching the tape as you go so that it sticks to itself.

4. Fold each 4" piece of blue ribbon in half widthwise. Fold down one top corner, creating a 45-degree angle. Beginning at top of unfolded end, sew running stitches along top edge, and diagonally to lower point. Pull up thread, gathering ribbon to 1½"; knot thread. Open petal.

7

7. Cut one selvedge from the yellow grosgrain. Pull out five bunches of thread. Fold each bunch in half and glue one bunch into the center of each flower.

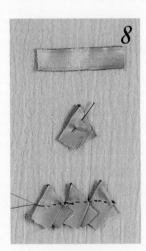

8

8. Cut six 2" pieces of blue taffeta for buds. Remove wires. Overlap the ends of each piece at a 45-degree angle and pin in place. Sew three petals together with small running stitches as shown in photo at left. Pull up thread tightly and join last petal to first; knot thread.

9. Cut twelve 2" pieces of green taffeta. Remove wires. Wrap a ribbon around bottom of bud, overlapping the ends. Turn top cut end under ¼" and stitch top selvedge to bottom of bud. Stitch side seam; knot thread. Sew running stitches along bottom selvedge. Insert a short length of green braid. Pull thread tight; knot thread. Finish flowers in same way, omitting stems. After making and attaching leaves, cover floral tape in same way, inserting different lengths of soutache braid before closing casing.

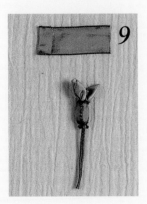

9

10

10. Cut ten 6" and three 8" pieces of ⅝" green taffeta. Fold each piece in half widthwise. Machine-sew from top corner of cut end to bottom corner of folded end; backstitch and clip thread. Trim and seal seams the same as for 3" petals. Open ribbon. Attach small leaves to wire stem of flower with 2" of floral tape. Arrange pieces on muslin and stitch in place.

Blue Flag Iris

Prostrate Bluet

Houstonia serpyllifolia

More than two dozen species of bluets are found in North America, covering large patches of woodland and meadow. The bluet blooms from April to July, depending on species and location.

MATERIALS

- 2½ yards of ⅝"-wide or 1"-wide blue wire-edge taffeta

- 1 yard of ⅝"-wide green wire-edge taffeta

- Nine 1" squares of buckram

- 24" of green soutache braid for stems

- 4" of 1"-wide white grosgrain

- 2" of 1"-wide brown grosgrain

- Nine yellow stamens

- 8" x 10" piece of natural muslin

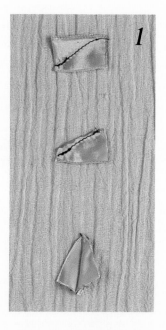

1. Cut thirty-six 2" pieces of blue taffeta and nine 1" squares of buckram for nine flowers. Set aside buckram squares. Remove wires from ribbon pieces. Fold each piece in half widthwise. Using a straight stitch, machine-sew from top corner of cut end to bottom corner of folded end. Backstitch and clip thread. Trim ribbon to ⅛" from seam. Seal raw edges with clear nail polish to prevent raveling. Open up ribbon to a small triangular petal.

2. Use a running stitch to join four petals, stitching ⅛" from the straight edges. Pull thread tight to gather petals, then join the last petal to the first; knot the thread. Sew the petals to the center of a buckram square. Make nine flowers.

3. Cut the white grosgrain into 2" pieces. Cut one selvedge edge from each white piece and from the brown piece, and pull out threads. Cross two bunches of 8 to 10 white threads in the center of each flower. Sew in place, stitching through the buckram. Trim threads to ¾". Stitch one bunch of 8 to 10 brown threads in center of white threads. Trim to ½".

4. Finish each flower with one small yellow stamen, carefully glued to the center. Trim buckram close to stitching on back.

5. Cut nine 2" pieces from remaining blue taffeta. Referring to photo at left, sew small running stitches from one top corner to bottom selvedge. Sew along the bottom selvedge for about 1½", then continue sewing up to top selvedge. Pull up thread, gathering ribbon to ¼" and overlap the ends. Cut three 2" pieces of green taffeta. Remove wires. Wrap ribbon around bottom of bud, overlapping the ends. Turn top cut end under ¼" and stitch the top selvedge to the bottom of the bud. Blind-stitch the side seam; knot thread. Sew running stitches along the bottom selvedge of casing. Pull up gathers and knot thread.

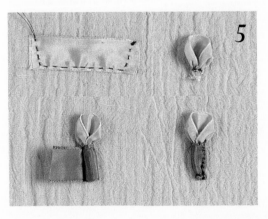

7. Cut two 3", 4", and 5" pieces each of green soutache braid. Sew to muslin with flowers and leaves.

6. Cut remaining 30" of green ribbon into ten 3" pieces. Fold each ribbon in half widthwise. Fold down the top corner at the folded end to rest just above the lower selvedge. Beginning at the bottom corner of the cut end, sew up to top selvedge. Sew along the top selvedge, then down to the bottom corner of the folded edge. Pull up the thread slightly. Open up the layers and move the gathers to give the leaf a pear shape. Backstitch; knot and clip thread.

Prostrate Bluet

Purple Coneflower

Echinacea purpurea

Coneflowers can be found all over North America from late summer to early autumn. They appear to have antiviral and antibiotic effects. The sharp-pointed bracts of the flower are named after the Greek "echinos" or hedgehog.

MATERIALS

- 1¼ yards of 1"-wide pink shaded wire-edge taffeta (flower A)

- 2½ yards of 1"-wide light green/dark pink shaded wire-edge taffeta (flowers B and C)

- 1¼ yards of 1"-wide burgundy/dark green shaded wire-edge taffeta (flower D)

- 20" of ⅝"-wide brown grosgrain for center

- 20" of ⅝"-wide burgundy grosgrain for center

- 27" of 1"-wide green shaded wire-edge taffeta for leaves

- Four 3" squares of buckram

- 28" of green soutache braid for stems

- 8" x 10" piece of natural muslin

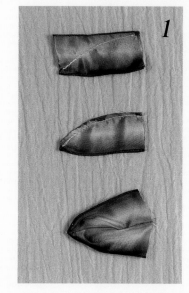

1. For each flower, cut eleven 4" pieces from one of the shaded pink or burgundy taffetas. For flower A, fold each piece in half widthwise with the light pink shading at the bottom. For flowers B and C, fold each piece in half widthwise with the dark pink shading at the bottom. For flower D, fold each piece in half width-wise with the burgundy shading at the bottom. Beginning at the top corner of the cut end, hand- or machine-sew just under the top selvedge for about ½", then sew diagonally to the bottom corner of the folded end. Back-stitch for ½"; knot and clip thread. Trim ribbon to within ⅛" of the seam. Apply clear nail polish to the cut edges to prevent fraying.

2. Using running stitches about ¼" above the cut ends, join the eleven petals. Pull the thread tightly to gather, and join the last petal to the first; knot and clip thread.

3. Attach the flower to the center of a buckram square and secure with several stitches at the previous gathering stitches. Attach the remaining flowers in same way.

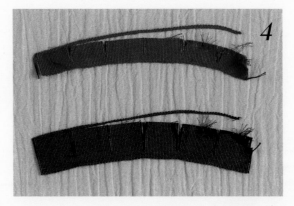

4. Cut four 5" pieces each of brown and burgundy ⅝" grosgrain. Cut off top selvedge from each piece. Make five ⅜"-deep clips, spacing them about ⅞" apart. Use a thick pin or an awl to fray each piece by pulling out threads, stopping ¼" above bottom selvedge.

5. Lay one piece of the frayed burgundy ribbon on top of the frayed brown ribbon and, beginning at one end, coil inward. Tack the selvedge as you coil, until all the ribbon is used. Finish the other three centers in the same way. Sew the coiled center through the ¼" unfrayed portion to the center of the flower and to the buckram with small blind-stitches. Trim buckram close to stitching in back.

6. Cut three 9" pieces of green taffeta. On each piece, fold down the top corners to rest just above the lower selvedge. Beginning at the cut end, sew a small running stitch up on the diagonal, along the top and down on the diagonal to the folded point. Pull up the thread, forming a pod shape. Open the layers into a leaf. Adjust the gathers towards the base, so the leaf resembles a pear. Backstitch; knot and clip thread.

7. Cut four 7" pieces of green braid. Sew to muslin with flowers and leaves.

Coneflower

Black-eyed Susan

Rudbeckia hirta

This prairie biennial with its flat daisylike flowers blooms from June through October in fields, prairies, and open woods. The North American native is easy to grow almost anywhere.

MATERIALS

- 3½ yards of ⅝"-wide yellow shaded wire-edge taffeta for three flowers and two buds

- 8" of 1"-wide green wire-edge taffeta

- 20" of ⅝"-wide green wire-edge taffeta

- 26" of green soutache braid

- 8" x 10" piece of muslin

- Three 3" squares of buckram

- 4" of black velvet tubing

- Three black velvet buttons

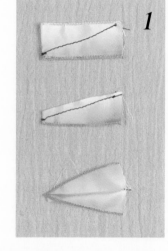

1. Cut forty 3" pieces of yellow taffeta. Fold each piece in half widthwise with the lighter shade on top. Hand- or machine-stitch a diagonal line from the top corner of the cut end to the the bottom corner of the folded end. Carefully trim the ribbon to ⅛" from the seam. Apply nail polish to the raw edges of the seam. Open the layers.

2. Using running stitches about ¼" above the cut ends, join ten petals. Pull the thread tightly to gather, and join last petal to the first; knot and clip thread. Sew the center of the flower to the center of a buckram square. Trim the buckram to within ¼" from the stitching. Glue a black velvet button to the flower center. Make three flowers.

3. Join five petals as in Step 2, however, make sure the seams are facing you. Gather into a bud but do not yet draw the thread tight. Cut two 2" pieces of black velvet tubing. Fold a piece of tubing in half and position the cut ends in the center of the bud. Pull the thread tightly to finish the bud and to secure the black velvet center. Make two buds.

4. Cut two 2" pieces of $\frac{5}{8}$" green taffeta. Remove the wires. Wrap ribbon around bottom of a bud, overlapping the ends. Turn top cut end under $\frac{1}{4}$" and stitch the top selvedge to the bottom of the bud. Blind-stitch side seam; knot thread. Cut one 2" and one 6" piece of green braid. Sew running stitches along bottom selvedge and insert one of the braid pieces. Pull thread tight around braid; backstitch and knot thread.

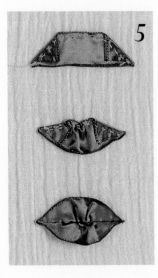

5. Cut the remaining $\frac{5}{8}$" green ribbon into four 4" pieces. Fold each 4" piece in half widthwise and fold down the top corners, letting them rest just above the lower selvedge. Begin to stitch diagonally on the cut-end side, then along the top edge, and down the diagonal of the other end. Pull up the threads to create a pod shape. Open the layers into a leaf. Adjust the gathers so the leaf is somewhat pear-shaped. Backstitch; knot and clip thread. Use the 8" piece of 1"-wide green ribbon to make one large leaf using the same technique as for the smaller leaves.

6. Cut three 6" pieces of green braid. Sew to muslin with flowers and leaves.

Black-eyed Susan

Morning Glory

Ipomoea purpurea

The common Morning Glory originated in tropical America and can be found in fields and along roadsides. The viny stems ("ipomoea" means wormlike!) wind their way up the stalks of other plants, seriously affecting such crops as corn, cotton, and soybeans.

MATERIALS

- 21" of 1½"-wide purple shaded wire-edge taffeta for two flowers and one bud

- 18" of 1½"-wide dark pink shaded wire-edge taffeta for one flower and two buds

- 8" of 1½"-wide light pink shaded wire-edge taffeta for one flower

- Four yellow stamens

- 20" of moss-green soutache braid for stems

- 28" of 1"-wide green wire-edge taffeta for leaves

- 6" of ⅝"-wide green wire-edge taffeta for casings

- 8" x 10" piece of natural muslin

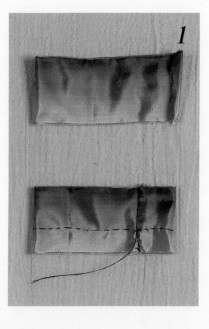

1. From the purple taffeta, cut two 8" pieces for two flowers and set aside the remaining 5" piece for a bud. From the dark pink taffeta, cut one 8" piece for one flower and set aside two 5" pieces for buds. Use the 8" piece of light pink taffeta for one flower. Fold each 8" piece in half widthwise and sew the raw ends together, using ½" seam allowances. Turn the seam allowances under ¼" to encase the edges. Sew two rows of running stitches around the ribbon, one row about ½" above the lighter edge and one just above the selvedge.

2. Begin pulling the threads to gather the bottom of the flower. Insert the stamen in the center; pull the bottom thread tightly around the stamen wire and knot. Secure the top thread when there's a ½" center opening left.

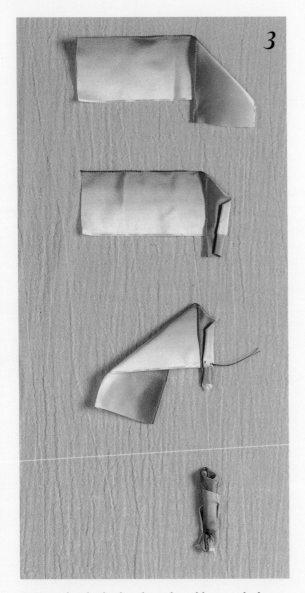

3

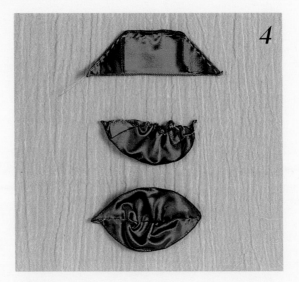

4

4. Cut four 7" pieces of 1"-wide green taffeta. Fold each piece in half widthwise. Fold down the top corners, letting them rest just above the lower selvedge. Beginning at the bottom corner of the cut end, sew running stitches to the top selvedge, then along the top, and then down to the other bottom corner. Pull the thread so the gathered edge measures about 2½". Open the layers to reveal a leaf. Adjust the gathers so the leaf is pear shaped. Back-stitch for about ½"; knot and clip the thread.

5. Cut two 10" pieces of green braid. Sew to muslin with flowers, buds, and leaves.

3. To make the buds, place the ribbon with the darker shading at the top and fold down one end so that ½" hangs below the bottom selvedge. Roll the end inward for two revolutions. Fold back the top selvedge of the free section, creating a long bias fold. Loosely roll the bud inwards until the bias fold becomes part of the bud. Secure the raw edge of the end to the base of the bud. Cut three 2" pieces of green 5/8" taffeta. Remove the wires. Wrap ribbon around the bottom of a bud, overlapping the ends. Turn top cut end under ¼" and stitch the top selvedge to the bottom of the bud. Blind-stitch side seam; knot thread. Sew running stitches along bottom selvedge and pull thread to gather closed; knot thread.

Morning Glory

Day Lily

Hemerocallis fulva & Hemerocallis flava

The buds of this native of Eurasia are edible and taste like green beans when cooked. Day lilies can be found from May through July along roadsides and in meadows. Hemerocallis, meaning "beautiful for a day," describes well the plant's bloom schedule.

MATERIALS

- 24" of gold/yellow, 12" of orange, 18" of peach, 12" of apricot, and 18" of lemon yellow ⅝"-wide shaded wire-edge taffeta for six flowers and two buds

- 12 yellow stamens

- 2 yards of ⅝"-wide moss-green wire-edge taffeta for leaves

- 8" x 10" piece of muslin

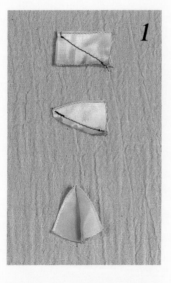

1. Cut all ribbons, except the green ribbon, into 2" pieces. Separate pieces according to color. You need six pieces for each flower. Fold the pieces in half widthwise and machine- or hand-sew from the bottom corner at the cut end to the top corner at the folded end. Backstitch, and clip thread. When using the shaded ribbon, position the darker shading at the bottom, then proceed in the same manner. Trim the excess ribbon ⅛" from the seam allowances and coat the raw edges with clear nail polish to prevent fraying.

2. Using running stitches, join six petals about ⅛" from their cut ends. Pull up the thread tightly, leaving a very small opening in the center, and join the last petal to the first petal. Do not yet knot the thread.

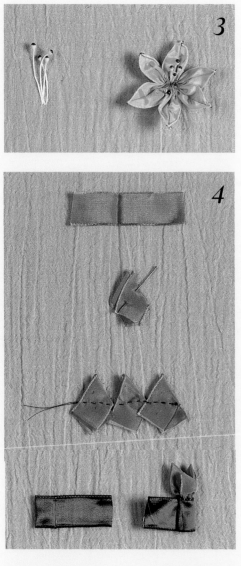

3. Fold two stamens in half and insert their folded ends through the small opening at the center of the petals. Let the folded end of the stamens extend from the bottom of the flower by ½". Now pull the thread even tighter to close the center completely; backstitch, and knot the thread.

4. Remove the wires from the selvedges of the remaining peach shaded pieces and lemon yellow pieces. Diagonally fold one end over the other end of each 2" piece, and pin in place. Using running stitches, join three bud petals. Pull up the threads tightly and join the last petal to the first; knot. For each flower, cut a 2" piece of green taffeta. Wrap this piece around the bud's base. Sew the top selvedge of the casing to the bud. Turn a ¼" hem at the end of the casing, and secure the seam with blind-stitches. Sew running stitches along the lower casing edge. Pull up the thread tightly; knot the thread.

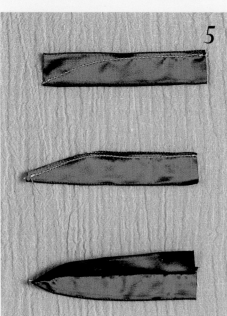

5. Cut the green ribbon into 6" to 8" pieces. Fold each piece in half widthwise. Machine- or hand-sew from the top corner of the cut end, along the top selvedge, and then down to the bottom corner of the folded end. Backstitch, and clip thread. Trim the excess ribbon to ⅛" from the seam and coat the raw edges with clear nail polish to prevent fraying.

6. Arrange pieces on muslin as shown below, or as desired, and stitch in place.

Day-Lily

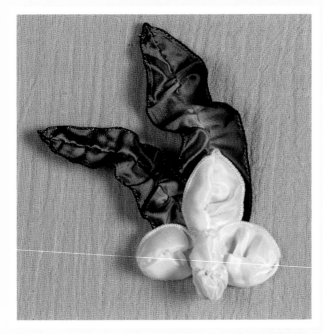

Showy Lady's Slipper

Cypripedium reginae

The Showy Lady's Slipper is the tallest of North American orchids. It is an endangered wildflower found in swamps and limestone sites, especially in the Great-Lake states. Many Lady's Slipper species have become rare in the wild due to the depradations caused by zealous plant hunters.

MATERIALS

- 24" of ⅝"-wide pink shaded wire-edge taffeta

- 2 yards of ½"-wide white wire-edge taffeta

- 2 yards of ⅝"-wide green shaded wire-edge taffeta

- 25" of ¼"-wide moss-green soutache braid

- Six 1" squares of buckram

- 8" x 10" piece of natural muslin

1. Cut six 3½" pieces from the white taffeta. Fold each piece in half width-wise, fold the top corners down to rest just above the lower selvedge. Sew running stitches up one side, along the upper selvedge, and down the other side. Pull up the thread until the gathered edge measures 1". Adjust and push the gathers towards the cut end so the petal will have a pear shape. Backstitch, and knot the thread.

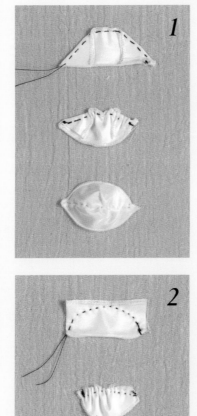

2. Cut twelve 3" pieces of white taffeta. Fold each piece in half width-wise. Sew small running stitches, starting at the bottom corner of the cut end, then arching around to the bottom corner of the folded end. Pull up the thread until the gathered edge measures about ¾". Backstitch, and knot thread. Carefully trim the excess ribbon to ⅛" from the seam, and apply clear nail polish to the raw edges to prevent fraying. Open up the petal.

3. Sew the base of the leaf from Step 1 to the center of the buck-ram. Next, join a pair of petals from Step 2 by overlapping their bases; sew to the base of the first leaf and to the buckram.

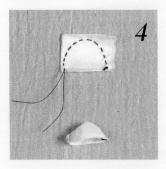

4. Cut six 2" pieces of white taffeta. Fold each piece in half widthwise. Sew small running stitches, starting from the bottom corner of the cut end, then arching around to the bottom corner of the folded end. Pull up the thread until the gathered edge measures about ¾". Backstitch, and knot thread. Trim the excess ribbon to ⅛" from the seam, and apply clear nail polish to the raw edges to prevent fraying. Open up the petal. Position and sew one end of the petal to the base of the three petals on the buckram.

5. Cut six 4" pieces of pink taffeta. Remove the wires. Fold each piece in half widthwise. Sew the cut ends together, using a ⅛" seam allowance. Knot and clip thread. Holding the layers together, sew running stitches along the darker selvedges. Pull up thread tightly; secure with a double knot. Turn the seam allowances to the inside. Sew running stitches along the lighter selvedges. To complete the slipper shape, pull up the thread tightly, but do not close; knot.

6. With the seam in back and the sewn-together ends upward, posi-tion the slipper from Step 5 on the base of the petals. Secure the ends to the center of the flower with several stitches. Place the point of the center petal just inside the opening of the slipper. Trim the buckram close to stitching in back.

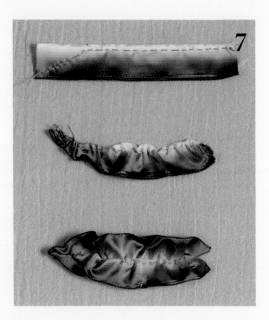

7. Cut nine 8" pieces of green taffeta. Fold each piece in half widthwise. Position the pieces with the darker shading at the bottom (for an interesting effect; reverse the coloration for several leaves). Starting at the top edge of the cut end, hand- or machine-stitch along the top selvedge for about 1", then down to the bottom corner of the folded end. Pull up the thread until the gathers measure about 3". Open the leaf. Push the gathers toward the cut end of the leaf. Backstitch; knot and clip the thread.

8. Cut green braid into a variety of lengths to fit muslin as shown below. Arrange pieces on muslin and stitch in place.

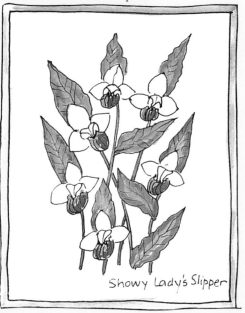

Showy Lady's Slipper

Step-by-Step

Hats for Dolls

Wouldn't you love to wear any one of these darling hats? Your dolls can! Fashion perky flowers out of precious bits of leftover ribbons, then plant them on the brim of a dainty sunbonnet or jaunty skimmer. Study the hat samples on the following pages—they're all shown with a sample strip of ribbons that make up the decoration—then try your hand at one or more of these coquettish head covers.

118

Buttercup

Ranunculus septentrionalis

The Swamp Buttercup grows in marshy areas, from New England to Maryland, and west to Kentucky and Missouri, flowering from April through July. It attracts butterflies and bees.

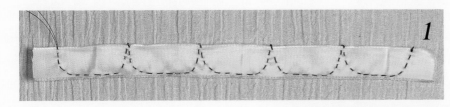

1. Starting $\frac{1}{2}$" from one cut end of the yellow taffeta, mark the lighter selvedge at $1\frac{1}{2}$" intervals. Remove the wire from the opposite selvedge. Beginning at the mark closest to one end and using double thread, take about three stitches toward the opposite edge; then sew along the edge; next take three stitches toward the next mark. Carry the fourth stitch around the selvedge. Continue to the end.

MATERIALS

- 9" of $\frac{5}{8}$"-wide yellow shaded wire-edge taffeta
- 1" of $\frac{5}{8}$"-wide golden yellow grosgrain
- 2" square of buckram

2. Pull the thread tightly until the gathered edge measures about 1". Join the first petal to the last petal, then pull the thread tighter. Knot the thread and and sew the flower to the buckram.

3. Cut one selvedge off the yellow grosgrain. Pull up, or fray, several threads. Position the threads across the middle of the flower and sew in place. Pull up several more threads and crisscross them with the other threads; sew to the center. Trim buckram close to stitching in back.

Dog Violet

Viola conspersa

This violet is found in meadows and damp woods from March through July, from Nova Scotia south through New England to Maryland and Georgia, then west to Alabama and north to Minnesota.

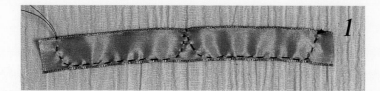

1

1. Cut a 5" length of taffeta and remove the wire from the bottom selvedge. Fold the ribbon in half to crease the center. Starting $\frac{1}{4}$" from one end and using double thread, take about three stitches toward the opposite edge; sew along the edge; then take three stitches toward the center crease. Carry the fourth stitch around the selvedge. Continue to the end.

MATERIALS

- 16" of $\frac{5}{8}$"-wide lavender wire-edge taffeta

- 1" of $\frac{5}{8}$"-wide yellow grosgrain

- 1" of $\frac{5}{8}$"-wide white grosgrain

- 2" square of buckram

2

2. Pull up the thread tightly and knot. Sew the gathers to the center of the buckram.

3

3. Cut three $3\frac{1}{2}$" pieces of lavender taffeta. Fold each piece in half widthwise. Sew running stitches from the top corner at the cut end down to the bottom corner at the folded end. Take a few backstitches, and clip the thread. Sew a few running stitches $\frac{1}{2}$" from the straight edge. Pull up the thread tightly and secure. Trim excess ribbon just below the gathers.

4. Attach two petals to the gathered portion of the flower and to the buckram. Position the gathered end of the third petal in the center of the flower, having the wrong side facing you and with the point upward. Sew the gathered edge in place. Fold the petal down.

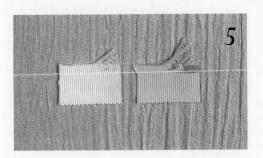

5. Cut a selvedge from the white grosgrain and pull out several threads. Bundle the threads and sew to the center of the flower. Repeat with the yellow grosgrain, but pull out and position more threads in the center. Trim the yellow threads close to the center. Trim the buckram close to the stitching in back.

 Position the dog violet at the edge of your hat's arrangement so the lower petal breaks the arrangement's line, creating an informal look.

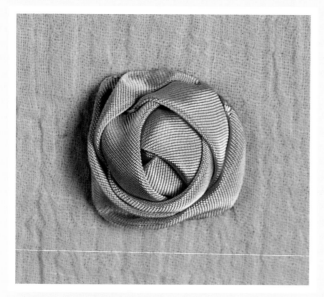

Chou Rose

Cabbage rose

The old-fashioned cabbage rose adds flair and fashion to a doll-hat bouquet. With its stable circular base, this flower functions well as an anchor point for your arrangement. Experiment with colors; overdyed ribbon especially creates an interesting effect when spiraled into shape.

MATERIALS

- 12" of ⅜"-wide pink shaded ribbon

- 1½" square of buckram

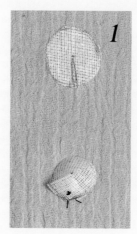

1. Cut a 1¼"-diameter circle from the buckram, and carefully slash from the edge to the center. Overlap the cut edges about ½" and stitch together along the edge, forming a cone shape.

2. Turn under ¼" at one end of the ribbon and place over the top of the cone. Using a knotted double thread and small running stitches, secure the ribbon to the buckram along the folded end. Let the needle and thread dangle in readiness for the next stitches.

The chou rose is excellent for filling in the base of your hat arrangement—it takes up a lot of space and then peeks out between more three-dimensional flowers.

3. Swing the ribbon counterclockwise a quarter turn, creating a diagonal fold on top of the cone. Do not flip the ribbon over—just swing it around! Tack across the width of the ribbon from the lower right corner to the upper right corner. Swing the ribbon counterclockwise another quarter turn (see photo), again creating a diagonal fold on top of the cone. Stitch across the width of the ribbon from the upper right corner to the upper left corner.

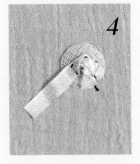

4. Make a third turn and stitch across the width again, gradually curving your line of stitches to follow the natural curve of the cone.

5. Make another turn and secure the ribbon across the width to the buckram. A small "window" should become visible in the center of the cone. Position your subsequent folds just enough below the previous folds so the folds ar not covered up—they form the petals of the rose. As you fold the ribbon, remember to always stitch across the width.

6. When the cone is completely covered with folds, trim the remaining length of ribbon and secure the end to the back of the buckram.

Wild Geranium

Geranium macuatum

Sometimes referred to as Cranesbill, the lavender to pink flower has a seed pod which resembles the bill of a crane. The species is found in forests, or where a forest once stood, from April through June, in Maine, and south to New England and Georgia; west to Tennessee, Missouri and Kansas; and north to Manitoba.

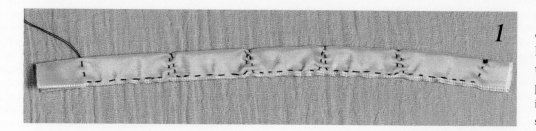

1

1. Cut one 8" piece and one 5" piece from the light pink taffeta. Remove the wires from both pieces. Fold the 8" piece in half lengthwise so the selvedges are at the bottom and the fold at the top. Beginning ¾" from one end, measure and mark five 1¼" spaces along the folded edge. Sew running stitches as shown in the photo, carrying the stitch over the top fold at each marked point.

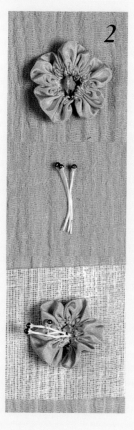

2

2. Pull the thread tightly, gathering the ribbon into a circle. Cut the stamens in half. Insert the stamens in the center of the circle, pull the gathers tighter, and secure stamens with several stitches. Join the ends of the ribbon circle and secure the thread. Sew the flower to the buckram.

MATERIALS

- 13" of 1"-wide light pink shaded taffeta

- 3 black-tipped stamens

- 2" inch square of buckram

- 1½" of ⅝"-wide green wire-edge taffeta for bud casing

3. Use the 5" pink taffeta to form three petals for the bud. The technique for making the petals is the same as for the flower. Pull the thread tightly and join the ends, omitting the stamens.

4. Remove both wires from the selvedges of the piece of green taffeta. Turn under a ¼" hem along one cut end.

5. Loosely wrap the green ribbon around the bud. Sew around the top selvedge of the green ribbon to attach the casing to the bud; backstitch. Sew down along the hemmed edge to the lower selvedge; backstitch. Sew running stitches around the lower selvedge. Draw up the thread tightly and knot. Secure the bud to the flower's buckram so it peeks out from behind the flower. Trim the buckram close to the stitching in the back.

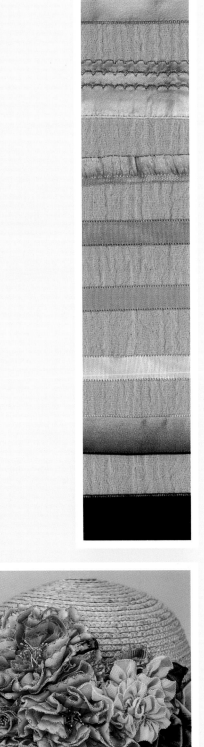

Have lots of different ribbons on hand so you can make one flower in many colors and sizes!

Mayweed & Wild Chamomile

Anthemis cotula & Matricaria

Mayweed looks like chamomile but has an unpleasant odor. Mayweed can be found along the roadside throughout America from June through October. Wild chamomile's leaves, when bruised, give off a fresh pineapple odor. The small daisylike flowerheads bloom in fields across the United States from May through September.

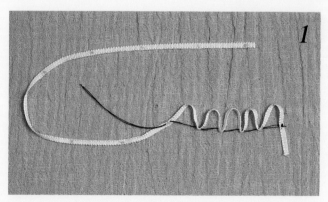

1. Cut the ⅛" yellow or white grosgrain into three 14" pieces. Measure and mark each piece of grosgrain at 1" intervals. For each flower, sew in and out at each mark, joining all thirteen points. Pull up the thread to gather the petals, and connect the first petal to the last, allowing a ⅛" space in the center for a fringed center.

MATERIALS

- 42" of ⅛"-wide yellow grosgrain for three mayweed OR 42" of ⅛"-wide white grosgrain for three chamomile

- 4" of ⅝"-wide yellow grosgrain

- Three 1" squares of buckram

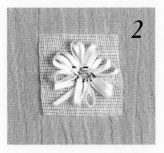

2. Place the flower on the buckram and sew the inside point of each petal to the buckram.

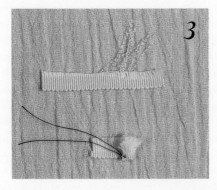

3. Cut two 2" pieces of yellow grosgrain. Fold the pieces in half lengthwise; cut on the fold. On one half of the ribbon and using a pin or awl, pull out threads to about ⅛" from the selvedge. Roll up the frayed grosgrain, securing it at the selvedge with small stitches as you go.

4. Place the yellow center in the opening of the flower and sew to the flower and to the buckram. Trim the buckram close to the stitches in back. If desired, you can cut the petals on the chamomile open to obtain more fringe-like petals.

For variety in the flowers' dimensions, sculpt the frayed center of the flowers and trim the petals.

Hat Tricks!

Most miniature blooms you see on the hats were created with narrower or lighter-weight ribbons and shorter ribbon lengths than are recommended for the larger flowers. For instance, to make a small zinnia, use 27" of ⅜"-wide grosgrain or other ribbon and treat as described on page 83.

To get more mileage out of your work, finish the back of the bouquet nicely by covering the buckram with a piece of felt.
A layer of thick iron-on interfacing in between the felt and the buckram will reinforce the backing even more. Now attach a pinback to the bouquet and you have a charming corsage to wear on your jacket lapel. Or glue it onto a barrette for a most romantic hair accessory!

Pods add interest to the overall arrangement and can even be used as flower centers! Follow the instructions in Step 5 on page 71 to make a basic pod, using ribbon of any width. A scalloped ribbon makes a darling pod. Or try a picot-edge ribbon in red for some rose hips.

Look through the pages of the Flower chapter to find leaves in all shapes and sizes. Make a collection of leaves using a variety of ribbons in different widths and colors. Then, using your flowers, pods, and leaves, and referring to the hat photographs in this chapter, compose your own mini-flower bouquet. When you're satisfied with the arrangement, tack each component to a wide strip or oval piece of buckram. When all the parts are attached, trim away the buckram, leaving a generous margin all around but making sure no buckram shows from the right side. You can now attach your bouquet to the hat.

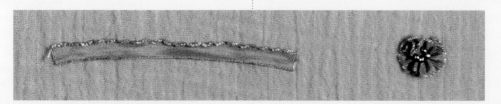

For the simplest of small flowers, gather up a short length of ribbon and sew the ends together. This type of flower functions well as a filler between other flowers on your hat and is a good way to use up leftover ribbon that's too short for anything else.

Generic four-and five-petal flowers are easily made by following the basic gathering technique used in Step 1 on page 124—the Wild Geranium. Use leftover stamens or grosgrain fringe for the centers. You can also tie a knot in a short length of rattail cord and attach the knot to the center of a flower.

Take a close look at the hats on each page of this Doll Hat chapter, and you'll notice that many of the hats sport dainty versions of the larger flowers used on the stunning wildflower quilt or shown in the general Flower chapter.

Decorate the brim with an interesting gathered or folded hatband. The brim on the hat shown right is festooned with a double serpentine treatment—one is stitched to the bottom of the brim, the other to the top. A velvet band of chevronned knife pleats encircles the bowl of the hat and is finished with a big bow in back. The ribbon-flower bouquet stylishly tops off this doll's delight.

Knife Pleat

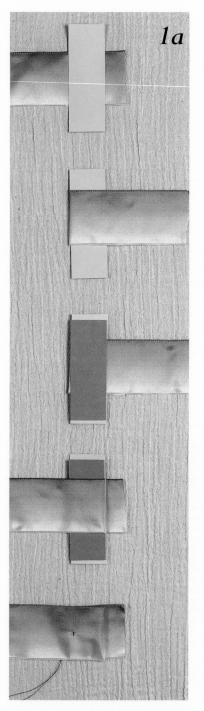

To make single knife pleats in any width ribbon, multiply the depth of the pleat by 3.5, then multiply the resulting number by the desired length of the pleated ribbon. Example: For a 24" hatband with 1" knife pleats you will need (1" x 3.5) x 24" = 84". (Add an additional ½" at each end for turning under.)

1a. Cut two 1" x 3" cardboard gauges. Place one gauge across the ribbon, ½" from one end. Fold the ribbon over the gauge and crease the ribbon at the fold (Fold 1). Place the second gauge on the ribbon, directly over the first. Fold the ribbon over the gauge again and crease the ribbon at the fold (Fold 2)—one pleat made. Remove the gauges. Use a knotted double thread to secure the center of the pleat with a single stitch. Let the needle hang free in back to tack each next pleat in the same way.

1b. To form the next pleat, place a gauge across the ribbon about ¼" to ½" from Fold 2. Fold the ribbon over the gauge and crease the ribbon. Place the second gauge on the ribbon, directly over the first one. Fold the ribbon over the gauge again and crease the ribbon. Remove the gauges and tack the pleat in the center, letting the needle hang free in back. Continue in this manner to the end of the ribbon. If desired, finish the ribbon by sewing a line of machine stitches along the center of the pleats. The gauges can be omitted once you've learned to gauge the depth of the pleats, which will speed up the process.

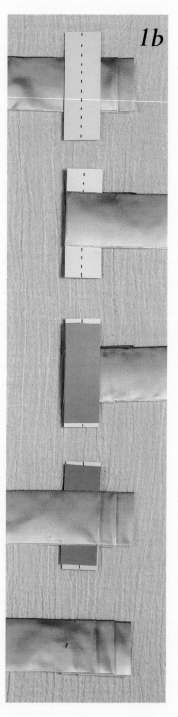

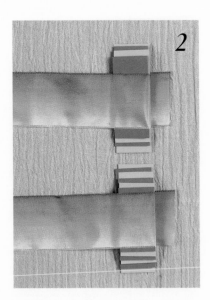

2. To make a band of double knife pleats, work as instructed for the single knife pleats, using four pieces of cardboard to make four folds right on top of each other. The result will be two pleats, one on top of the other. Tack through the center of both pleats.

To make a band of triple knife pleats, work as instructed for the single knife pleats, using six pieces of cardboard to make six folds right on top of each other. The result will be three pleats, one on top of the other. Tack through the center of all three pleats.

3. Variation: Use a 1½"-wide multicolor-striped ribbon to make a band of triple knife pleats. Position the needle and thread at the back of the first set of pleats and bring it up through the center base of the pleats. With the tip of the needle, catch the top two corners of the same pleat and push the needle down where you came up. Continue to the end of the ribbon.

4. Variation: Make a band of single knife pleats. Fold the top corners of each pleat onto the pleat, forming a Chevron. Position the needle and thread at the back of the first pleat and bring it up through the center base just above the second pleat. With the tip of the needle, catch the top layer of each corner slightly below the pleat and push the needle back down where you came up. Bring the needle up through the base of the second pleat and continue this process to the end of the ribbon. For more variety, fold down only one corner of each pleat, alternating the sides to create a pattern.

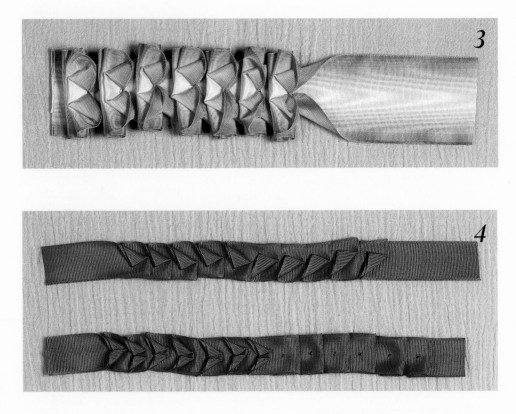

Box Pleat

To make a box pleat with a ½" depth in any width ribbon, multiply the depth of the pleat by 3, then multiply the resulting number by the desired length of the pleated ribbon. Example: For a 24" hatband with 1" box pleats you will need (1" x 3) x 24" = 72". (Allow an additional ½" at each end for turning under.)

1a. Cut four ½" x 3" cardboard gauges. Place one gauge straight across the ribbon, ½" from one end. Fold the ribbon over the gauge and crease the ribbon at the fold (Fold 1). Place the second gauge on the ribbon, directly over the first. Fold the ribbon over the gauge again and crease the ribbon at the fold (Fold 2)—you have now created the first half of the pleat. Turn the ribbon over.

1b. To form the second half of the pleat, place a third gauge across the ribbon right next to the first fold. Fold the ribbon over the gauge and crease the ribbon. Place the fourth gauge on the ribbon, directly over the third gauge. Fold the ribbon over the fourth and crease the ribbon. Remove the gauges. Use a knotted double thread to tack the two pleats together with a single stitch. Let the needle hang free in back to tack each succeeding pleat in the same way. Turn the ribbon and continue the process to the end of the ribbon. If desired, finish the ribbon by sewing a line of machine-stitches along the center of the pleats.

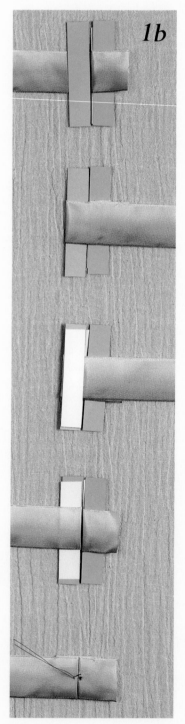

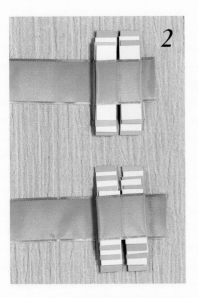

2. A triple box pleat consists of six pleats, three facing one direction and three facing the opposite direction. To calculate the length of ribbon needed, use the following formula: (depth of pleat X 5.5) x desired length. Example: For a 24" hatband with $1\frac{1}{2}$" pleats you will need (5.5 x 1.5") x 24" = 198" or $5\frac{1}{2}$ yards. (Allow an additional $\frac{1}{2}$" at each end for turning under.) Using $\frac{1}{2}$" x 3" gauges, make one triple knife pleat as directed in Step 2 on page 131. Turn the ribbon over and make another triple knife pleat. Tack the two sets of pleats together, turn the ribbon over, and continue the process to the end of the ribbon.

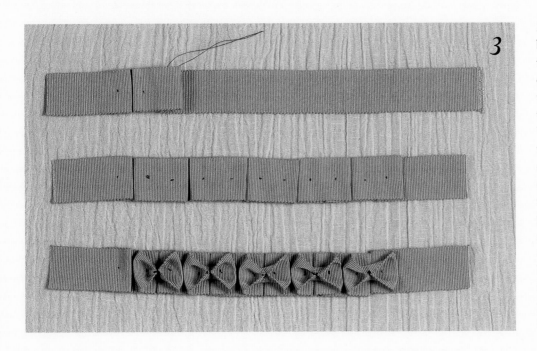

3. Variation: Make a band of box pleats, tacking the center of each individual fold without tacking the two folds together. With double thread, tack the center top edge of a pleat to the center bottom edge of the same pleat. Pull the thread tight so the edges meet in the center of the pleat; knot and clip the thread. Continue this process to the end of the ribbon.

Gathering

1. Fold the bottom right-hand corner of the ribbon toward the top selvedge so the cut end matches the top selvedge, and crease the fold. Fold the ribbon to the left so the top edges match, but do not crease the fold. Fold the ribbon down along its diagonal fold so the last fold matches the bottom selvedge, and crease the fold. Fold the ribbon to the left so the bottom edges match and do not crease the fold. Continue folding the ribbon in this way, creasing only the diagonal folds. Unfold the ribbon.

2. Using doubled thread, sew a running stitch across the ribbon, stitching along the crease marks.

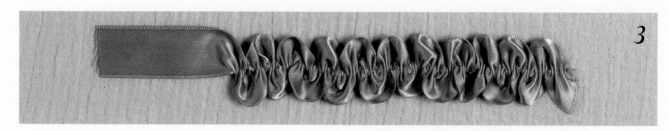

3. Pull the thread tight to gather the ribbon. Even out the gathers before securing the thread with a knot.

Serpentine Gathering

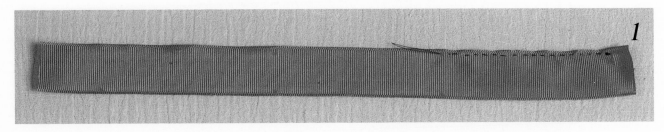

1. Use tailor's chalk to mark evenly spaced intervals across both selvedges of the ribbon. To determine the length of each interval, multiply the ribbon width by 3.5. Examples: 3.5 x 1" ribbon = 3.5" or 3½" intervals; 3.5 x 1.5" ribbon = 5.25" or 5¼" intervals.

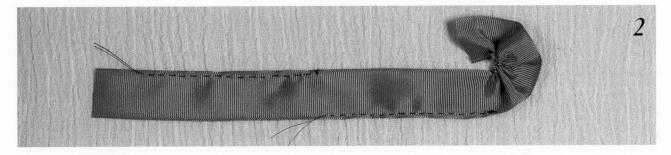

2. Using doubled thread, sew a running stitch across the top selvedge between the first and second marks. Pull the thread tight to gather the ribbon; knot and clip the thread in back. Sew a running stitch across the bottom selvedge between the second and third marks. Pull the thread tight to gather the ribbon; knot and clip the thread. Continue to stitch across the ribbon in the same way, remembering to alternate the edges.

3. To calculate the length of ribbon needed, use the following formula: (3.5 x ribbon width) x finished length. Example: For a 24" hatband using 1½"-wide ribbon you will need (3.5 x 1.5") x 24 = 126" or 3½ yards. (Allow an additional ½" at each end for turning under.)

Woven-Ribbon Technique

Selecting ribbons

Choosing ribbons of the same shade or closely related shades of one color is fairly easy—three, four, or five textures and widths of ribbon will make a lovely pattern. There are no hard and fast rules. To make your first weaving project easier, choose all ribbons of 1" width. If you feel adventurous, select ribbons of varying widths, say $\frac{1}{2}$" to $1\frac{1}{2}$". Weaving is a wonderfully creative way to use up leftover ribbon—if you have long lengths you can make a sizeable pillow top, and with short lengths you can make a small boxtop cover, purse, or mini pillow. To cover a large item with woven-ribbon fabric, draw ribbon-simulating guidelines on your pattern with a variety of widths in between the lines. Measure the lengths of the pretend ribbons, then double the amounts to make sure you have enough ribbon to weave in the other direction.

MATERIALS

- Variety of ribbons

- Iron-on interfacing

- Large piece of foamcore board

- Sewing supplies

1. With the adhesive side up, secure the interfacing with pins to the foamboard at corners. Place the first ribbon at an angle on the interfacing and pin at the beginning and the end. Continue laying out ribbons above and below the first ribbon, pinning as you go and keeping them closely aligned and parallel, to cover the entire piece of interfacing.

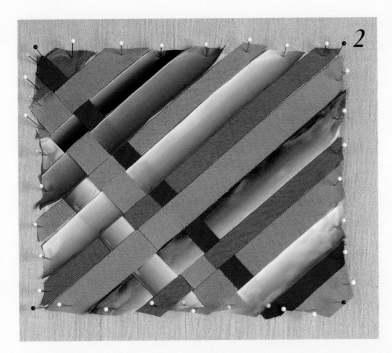

2. Starting in one corner, weave a long ribbon through the completed first layer and secure the ends with pins. Then continue weaving ribbons above and below this center ribbon, making sure the ribbons align, leaving no gaps.

3. With your iron on the steam setting and a damp cloth over the woven-ribbon fabric, press the iron on the fabric in an up and down motion, fusing the ribbons to the interfacing. Fold back the pressing cloth and remove the pins from one edge only; replace the cloth and press that edge. Repeat with the other edges. Turn the woven-ribbon fabric over and carefully press the back.

Making sure your purse, boxtop, or pillow pattern includes a generous seam allowance, place the pattern on the woven-ribbon fabric and lightly draw around it. Stitch on the drawn pattern line(s). Trim away the excess ribbon ends.

Frivolité

Spruce up a brass doorknob or curtain tieback with a wonderful whimsy called a frivolité. Combine a cocarde and galette, add a few bows, and voilá—instant charm!

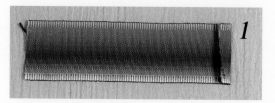

1. Cut a 3-yard length of 1¾" shaded grosgrain. Turn under ½" of ribbon at one end.

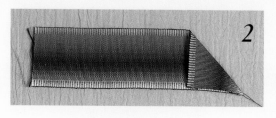

2. Turn the folded edge down so it rests on the bottom selvedge, forming a triangle. Using a knotted double thread, sew the edges together; knot the thread.

MATERIALS

- 6½ yards of 1¾"-wide shaded French grosgrain

- 16" of 1½"-wide picot-edge ribbon for loop

- 8" picot-edge ribbon for first bow

- purchased tassel

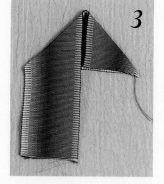

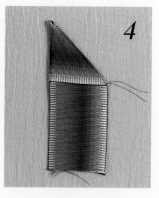

3. Fold the left end of the ribbon down so another triangle is created. At the center, leave about a ⅛" space so the selvedges from both the left and the right sides of the ribbon almost meet.

4. Fold the left triangle over the right triangle so the diagonal edges match. Secure the corner with a stitch and knot the thread, but do not cut it; let the needle and thread hang from the ribbon.

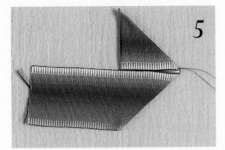

5. To form the next triangle, fold the length of ribbon upward to the bottom of the top triangle; leave a ⅛" gap, and crease the fold.

9. Turn the second cocarde over. The flat side is now facing up. Using double thread, sew running stitches through the center of the folds.

6. Fold the ribbon up, covering the top triangle. The ribbon should now look like the ribbon in Step 2.

7. Repeat Steps 3–6 until 31 points have been made. Turn under the final edge about ½" and secure with hidden stitches. Pull up the thread firmly and backstitch about every two points.

10. Pull up the thread until the ribbon forms a cup shape. Knot and cut the thread.

11. Sew running stitches through all the points that are sticking straight up. Pull thread up tightly until you have the same size center opening as on the reverse side. Knot and cut thread.

8. Join the first triangle to the last triangle to close the circle, making one cocarde. Use the remaining French grosgrain to make a second cocarde with 34 points.

12. Flatten the ribbon between your hands to form a doughnut or "galette" shape, pulling and pushing the folds until they lie down smoothly. Sew the edges of the center openings together.

13. Thread the galette onto the 16" length of 1½"-wide ribbon. Sew the ribbon ends together. Neatly attach the cocarde to the front of the hanging ribbon, just above the galette. Decorate the frivolité with a big bow at the top. Sew a tassel to the bottom of the galette, concealing the hanging loop in one of the folds.

Sources

ARTEMIS
179 High St.
South Portland, ME 04106
(207) 741-2509, Fax (207) 741-2497
Hand-dyed bias silk ribbons
Distributor of Hanah Silk
Retail and wholesale

BELL'OCCHIO
8 Brady St.
San Francisco, CA 94103
(415) 864-4048, Fax (415) 864-2626
New and vintage ribbons, millinery flowers
(French silk)
Retail

BRIMAR, INC.
1500 Old Deerfield Rd., Suite 5
Highland Park, IL 60035
(847) 831-2120, Fax (847) 831-3531
Tassels, cording, braids, metallic ribbons
Retail, wholesale, catalog available

BRITEX
146 Geary St.
San Francisco, CA 94108
(415) 392-2910, Fax (415) 392-3906
Fabric, buttons, ribbons, trims, buckram
Retail

CAMELA NITSCHKE RIBBONRY
119 Louisiana Ave.
Perrysburg, OH 43551
(419) 872-0073, Fax (419) 872-0073
Web address: http://www.ribbonry.com
Woven ribbons from France, wire-edge ribbons,
Mokuba ribbons, books, videos, kits, buckram,
stamens
Retail, wholesale, catalog available

ELSIE'S EXQUISIQUES
22691 Lambert St., Suite 513
Lake Forest, CA 92630
(714) 837-1885, Fax (714) 837-1886
Orders only: (800) 742-SILK
Ribbons, trims, miniature flowers, stamens, silk,
miniature grosgrain
Retail, wholesale, catalog available

A FINE ROMANCE
2912 Hennepin Ave. South
Minneapolis, MN 55408
(612) 822-4144, Fax (612) 822 9773
New and vintage ribbons, stamens, buckram
Retail

GARDNER'S RIBBON AND LACE
2235 E. Division
Arlington, TX 76011
(817) 640-1436
Ribbons, trims, buttons, lace
Retail and wholesale

LACIS
2982 Adeline Ave.
Berkeley, CA 94703
(510) 843-7178, Fax (510) 843-5018
Lace and lace supplies, ribbons, tassels, stamens,
beads
Retail, wholesale, catalog available

M & J TRIMMING COMPANY
1008 and 1014 6th Ave.
New York, NY 10018
(212) 391-9072
Trims, braids, ribbons, beaded appliques, fringes
Retail and wholesale

Nancy's Sewing Basket
2221 Queen Anne Ave. North
Seattle, WA 98109
(206) 282-9112, Fax (206) 282-7321
Fabric, supplies, ribbon
Retail

MKB
561 7th Ave.
New York, NY 10018
(212) 221-6663
Mokuba ribbons, call for distributors
Wholesale only

Ruban et Fleur
8655 Sepulveda Blvd.
Westchester, CA 90045
(310) 641-3466, Fax (310) 641-1211
Wired ribbon, stamens, jacquard ribbon, buckram
Retail, wholesale, catalog available

Tail of the Yak
2632 Ashby Ave.
Berkeley, CA 94705
(510) 841-9891
New and vintage ribbon, fabric flowers, leaves,
organzas, velvets
Retail

Tinsel Trading Company
47 West 38th St.
New York, NY 10018
(212) 730-1030, Fax (212) 768-8823
Antique trims, braids, ribbons, trims,
1900s metallic trims
Retail, wholesale, video, catalog available

YLI Corporation
PO Box 420-747
San Francisco, CA 94142
Fax (415) 255-2329
Pure silk ribbon, thread, yarn
Retail, wholesale, catalog available

Tallina's
15791 SE Highway 224
Clackamas, OR 97015
(503) 658-6148
Retail, wholesale, catalog available

Catan Floral
17647 Foltz Ind. Pkwy.
Strongsville, OH 44136
(800) 321-1494, Fax (216) 572-9954
Large craft supply store
Retail, no mail order

Index

Q indicates the flower is
used in the quilt.
H indicates miniature
flowers for hats.

THE RIBBONRY

Many thanks to my husband, Steve Nitschke —my mentor, photographer, and best friend. Thank you also to all the other members of my family for their patience and support.

I would like to thank my staff at The Ribbonry: Alice Croy, Jan Niles, Natalie Tallon, Marge Tiefenbach, and Gloria Weller.

Thanks also to Liz Berry, Hazel Hayden, Roger Zielinski, Jane Hess, Charlie Hess, and Ed Hess.

In France, I would like to thank: Madame Besse, Monsieur Faure, the Museum of Art and Industry in St. Etienne, and the Bibliothèque Nationale in Paris.

Camela